The Best in Baseball

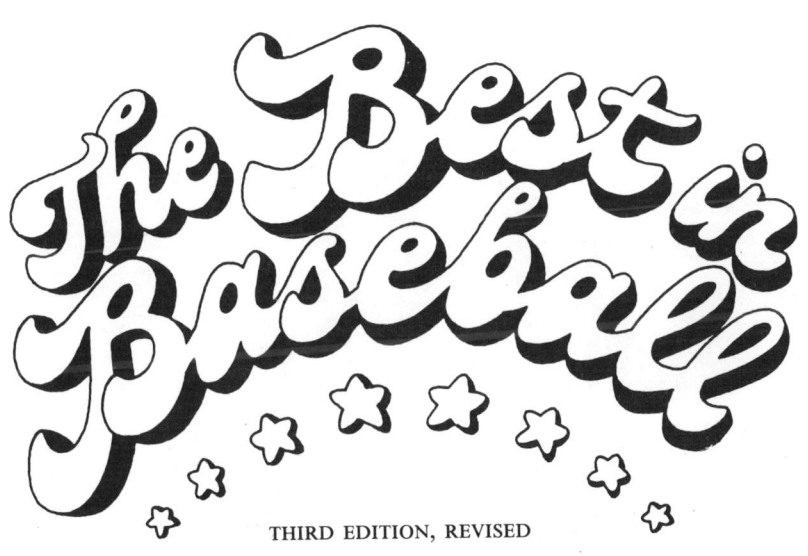

THIRD EDITION, REVISED

By Robert H. Shoemaker

THOMAS Y. CROWELL COMPANY
New York

Copyright © 1974, 1962, 1954, 1949 by Robert H. Shoemaker
All rights reserved. Except for use in a review, the reproduction or utilization of this work in any form or by any electronic, mechanical, or other means, now known or hereafter invented, including xerography, photocopying, and recording, and in any information storage and retrieval system is forbidden without the written permission of the publisher. Published simultaneously in Canada by Fitzhenry & Whiteside Limited, Toronto.

MANUFACTURED IN THE UNITED STATES OF AMERICA

Library of Congress Cataloging in Publication Data Shoemaker, Robert Hilles, 1911– The best in baseball. SUMMARY: Profiles of twenty-one baseball greats provide an outline of baseball history. 1. Baseball—Biography—Juv. lit. [1. Baseball—Biography] I. Title.
GV865.A1S513   1974   796.35/092'2 [D] [920]
73-20442   ISBN 0-690-00314-5

10   9   8   7   6   5   4   3   2   1

ST. LEONARD SCHOOL
MUSKEGO, WISCONSIN

This book is dedicated
to Kenny

Acknowledgments

For furnishing much of the material on which this book is based, the author is indebted to Charles M. Segar, Secretary-Treasurer of the Major Leagues; Earl J. Hilligan, manager of the American League Service Bureau; Connie Mack, late manager of the Philadelphia Athletics; Garry Schumacher, of the New York Giants; Edward T. Fitzgerald, of the Detroit Tigers; Marshall C. Samuel, of the Cleveland Indians; James J. Long, of the Pittsburgh Pirates; Charles B. Cozadd of Detroit; Frank Graham, Jr., of the Brooklyn Dodgers; Wayne Chandler, of the Houston Astros; Robert O. Fishel, of the New York Yankees; Larry Shenk, of the Philadelphia Phillies; and numerous ball players and friends of ball players, who contributed many of the anecdotes.

Other invaluable sources were microfilms of *The New York Times* in the New York Public Library; the library of the *New York Herald-Tribune*; *The Sporting News* and its *Official Baseball Guide*, and other record books; histories of baseball clubs; and various autobiographies and biographies of players, newspaper and magazine articles, and standard sports reference books.

Contents

Greatest of Them All: Ty Cobb	1
The One and Only: Babe Ruth	16
Saga of a Rajah: Rogers Hornsby	32
Connie's Kids: Al Simmons and Mickey Cochrane	49
After the Babe: Lou Gehrig	72
King Carl: Carl Hubbell	85
Not So Dizzy: Dizzy Dean	99
Indian Chief: Bob Feller	117
Yankee Clipper: Joe DiMaggio	127
A Pair of Aces: Stan Musial and Ted Williams	138

The Pride of Milwaukee: Warren Spahn	156
Pioneer on the Base Paths:	
Jackie Robinson	167
Joy in Philly: Robin Roberts	179
Yankee Siege Gun: Mickey Mantle	194
Wings on His Feet: Willie Mays	207
In Quest of the Magic Number:	
Hank Aaron	219
"Peace in Right Field": Roberto Clemente	230
Carlton Conquers All: Steve Carlton	242
Red Powerhouse: Johnny Bench	252
Index	263

Greatest of Them All: Ty Cobb

Baseball historians, statisticians, and just plain experts are generally agreed on one point: Ty Cobb was the greatest player who ever lived. They'll argue indefinitely the relative merits of Stan Musial and Ted Williams, Dizzy Dean and Bob Feller, Carl Hubbell and Warren Spahn; but when it comes to the Georgia Peach, there's no argument. Ty was in a class by himself, the undisputed top man of his day; and so far, no man has even come close to challenging him.

The scourge of the American League for twenty-four years, Cobb used his tremendous natural ability, a savage, flaming spirit, and high-grade intelligence to produce the greatest set of records the baseball world has ever known. Let's take a quick look at some of the cold figures. In almost a quarter-century of major-league ball, Cobb played 3,033 games; had a lifetime batting average of .367; led his league in batting twelve times; three times hit over .400; scored 2,244 runs; made 4,191 base hits; and stole 892 bases, 96 of them in one season alone.

The figures are impressive, but they don't tell the whole story of Ty Cobb. He was a snarling, fighting ball player, and once the umpire called "Play ball!" he became a ruthless, driving force on the diamond. He wanted one thing and one thing only—victory. And sometimes, it is said, he didn't care how he got it. Many baseball-loving fathers still tell their sons and grandsons the thrilling stories of Cobb tearing down the base paths with his sharpened spikes glittering in the sun. Baseball was a rough sport in Cobb's day—they played for keeps.

A slim, well-built athlete, Cobb stood a little over six feet and weighed, in his prime, around 175 pounds. He had blue eyes and light-colored hair, and an inexhaustible supply of nervous energy that kept him going at full tilt through every minute of every game.

He was utterly fearless, and battled with opposing players, his own teammates, umpires, and fans. He must have had a frightful disposition, particularly in his early days, for he was hated and feared throughout the league. But he was great. His speed and daring on the base paths would often throw an infield into a panic of errors. More than once in his brilliant career he scored all the way from first base on a single, or took two bases on a sacrifice bunt.

It is said that some infields developed what they considered the only formula for halting the rampaging Cobb. When he was on first and started to steal second, the catcher would whip the ball to third. As one backstop put it, "We outsmarted him; we held him to one base." It may have been pretty clever at that—for let an infielder fumble or hesitate even momentarily and the flying Cobb would be off for the next base. And with his terrific speed and skillful sliding, the chances were good he'd make it.

Ty Cobb may be just a name in the record book to present-day fans, but to old-timers who were boys at Philadelphia's Shibe Park in the '20's, and no doubt at every other ball field in the American League, the fiery Georgian was a very real menace. As he led his swaggering Detroit Tigers onto the playing field he was invariably greeted with boos and jeers, and he invariably answered with a snarl and, often as not, a ringing base hit.

One day he was having a bad time of it. A nondescript Philadelphia pitcher was enjoying a good day, and the "Georgia Peach" had been retired his first three times at bat. The A's were two runs ahead and fans were having a fine time at Cobb's expense. But Philadelphia's hurler weakened suddenly in the eighth inning and filled the bases with two out. Up to the plate stepped Cobb and slammed the first pitch to right field for a double, clearing the bases. Ty easily streaked into third on the throw to the plate and stood on the bag, smiling grimly.

Another day—ninth inning: Cobb stands on first with the tie-breaking run. He adjusts his cap, steps off the bag—a big lead. The pitcher watches him nervously, throws to first base. Cobb slides back safely. He takes the big lead again; he seems to be sneaking farther and farther along the line. The sweating pitcher throws to the plate, Cobb breaks for second, the batter swings—hit-and-run! It's a short single to center field. Cobb, running with the wind, races around second. The center fielder blazes the ball to third. But everybody's jittery when Cobb is running. The throw is wide of the bag and Cobb hook-slides in safely. But wait a minute. The third baseman has knocked the ball down; it rolls a few feet away. Like a flash Cobb is up on his feet and tearing for the plate. The third sacker finally grabs the ball and fires it home. Cobb and the ball are streaking for the plate. It's close, but Cobb slams into the catcher, who drops the ball. Cobb scores again for Detroit. It's the winning run, and a few minutes later the Athletic fans file silently out of the park. What can you do with a fellow like that?

There was only one man who could stop the Georgia Peach, and that was Father Time. It took him quite a while. After twenty-two years with the

Tigers, Ty came to the Philadelphia Athletics in 1927. And although he was then close to his forty-first birthday, he played 134 games and hit .357! He played 94 games the following year and hit .323, to wind up the greatest career in the history of the national pastime.

The saga of Ty Cobb began December 18, 1886, in Narrow Banks County, Georgia. Tyrus Raymond was the son of State Senator W. H. Cobb, and as a boy had the advantages of social position and education. Most of his boyhood was spent in Royston, Georgia, where the Senator, later a superintendent of schools, maintained another home in addition to the country place in Narrow Banks.

Ty's baseball career gained some momentum through the help of a local Methodist minister who was a former ball player himself. He agreed to coach the boys' team and in return exacted a promise of regular church attendance. The plan apparently worked well for all concerned. The team won ball games, and its members showed up for Sunday services.

Cobb was only eighteen when he landed a job, through the good offices of his friend the minister, with Augusta, of the South Atlantic League. But he didn't last long. The story goes that he came up to the plate in an important game and received orders to lay down a bunt. Instead, he walloped the ball over the fence for a home run—and was fired for disobeying orders.

However that may be, he played briefly with Anniston, Southeastern League, and then went back to Augusta when that club had a change of managers. In the spring of 1905 the Detroit Tigers trained in Augusta, and they soon got to know the hotheaded young Cobb. In games between the two squads, the major leaguers took great delight in teasing Cobb and watching him splutter and curse. No matter that it was just an exhibition game; Cobb fought as though a World Series were hanging on the result.

The Tiger players all but forgot about Cobb when the major-league season got under way. But midway through the schedule they were hit by a series of injuries, and the next thing they knew, the obstreperous youngster had been called up from Augusta and was right in their midst.

Rookies had a hard time of it in those days. There was no coddling of potential stars; the older men, fearing the loss of job and income, did their best to discourage any promising newcomers. "You had to be tough," Cobb often said in later years.

Ty Cobb's debut in the majors came on August 30, 1905. Facing New York's Jack Chesbro, one of the top hurlers of all time, the bad-tempered rookie pinch hitter sneered and blasted out a double which won the ball game, 5–3.

That was the beginning; the end was a long way off. The next year Cobb played 97 games and hit .320, and in 1907 he was a fixture in the Detroit outfield. Not yet twenty-one years old, the fiery young Georgian won the American League batting crown with a .350 average.

The 1907 American League race was a thriller and wound up in a tremendous battle between the Athletics and Tigers. The A's were leading by three percentage points when the Tigers came into Philadelphia for three games. Detroit won the first game narrowly, 5-4, and the next day, Saturday, it rained. This meant a double-header on Monday (Sunday baseball was prohibited in Philadelphia), and it provided Cobb with one of the big thrills of his career.

The Philadelphians got away to a fast start and were leading by the apparently safe margin of 7-1 when the Tigers came up in the seventh inning. Taking advantage of an error and the pitcher's wildness, the Tigers picked up four runs and were back in the ball game. But when each team scored once in the eighth, the Tigers were still trailing by two runs. Came the ninth inning, and Sam Crawford singled for the Tigers. Young Ty Cobb then slugged a home run over the right-field wall to tie the score. It was one of three hits he gathered in this vital game.

From then on there was even more excitement. Each team scored once in the tenth. Harry Davis, of Philadelphia, hit into the crowd lining center field in the fourteenth for what appeared to be a ground-rule double. The Detroit outfielder, however, claimed spectators had interfered with his attempted catch of the ball, and the umpires backed him up, calling

Davis out. The Athletics went wild with rage and a fight broke out on the field. Order was finally restored, and the game went on through the seventeenth inning, when the umpires called the game because of darkness.

As a result of this stalemate, the Tigers left Philadelphia with a half-game lead, and they held it to the finish, to give Detroit its first pennant since 1887.

The World Series, however, was a different story—an unfortunate experience for all the Tigers, including their youthful American League batting champion. Facing a great Chicago Cub team which featured the hurling of Mordecai ("Three-Finger") Brown, Ed Reulbach, Jack Pfeister, and Orvie Overall, the best the Tigers could do was tie the first game at 3–3.

Thereafter, they lost four straight and the Series. It was an especially sad occasion for the Detroit siege gun, Ty Cobb. Hitless in the first game, Ty got one blow in each of the remaining games to assemble a lowly .200 batting average.

Ty appeared in three World Series in succession, and in a way it is unfortunate that these opportunities came so early in his career. At that, he did well enough in 1908 when the Tigers again bowed to the Cubs. Ty picked up seven hits for a .368 average, but only in the third game did he look like the terror of the American League. Then he hit three singles and a double and stole two bases as Detroit gained its lone victory of the Series.

The year 1909 found the Tigers locked in another of their vicious struggles with Connie Mack's Philadelphia Athletics. During a midsummer game, Cobb ripped into third and accidentally spiked Frank Baker, the A's' third baseman. Philadelphia fans became excited, claiming Cobb had done it purposely to cripple the team. Cobb denied the charge and said it was up to the baseman to protect himself at all times.

The result of this storm of protest was that when the Tigers came to the City of Brotherly Love for a late-season series, Cobb had to be escorted by police to and from the ball park. But the ill will of the Philadelphia fans bothered Cobb not in the least. He hit and ran with his usual abandon, and Detroit won its third straight pennant. Ty's .377 gave him his third straight batting crown, and he also led the league in home runs. His total was nine, a far cry from Babe Ruth's records—but this was a different era.

Detroit had won another pennant, but there were the same old headaches in the World Series. The Tigers couldn't win for love nor—what was more important—money. This time it was the Pittsburgh Pirates who upset Cobb, Crawford & Co., but it took them seven games to do it—and the Pirates knew they had been in a fight.

As usual, Ty Cobb had some difficulty with National League hurling. At bat 26 times, he was credited with just six hits. And although he had not yet reached his peak of perfection at bat or on the base paths, this was his last chance in a World Series.

By this time, the young slugger's brash tactics had made him unpopular throughout the league, and this all but cost him his precious batting title in 1910. All through the season, in which the Detroit club dropped to third place, Cobb had a stiff contest for batting honors with Larry Lajoie, Cleveland's fine hitter. An automobile company announced it would present a car to the winner. With Cobb and Lajoie practically tied for the lead, the Indians played a double-header with the St. Louis Browns on the last day of the season.

According to legend, the St. Louis manager instructed his third baseman to play back on the grass whenever Lajoie came up to the plate. Larry was credited with eight hits on that afternoon, and six of them were bunts along the third-base line. This was a disagreeable business, to say the least, and it was followed by a quick investigation which apparently got nowhere. Nevertheless, when the official averages were announced, it was found that Cobb, with .385, led Lajoie by one point. The automobile company did the right thing: it gave cars to both sluggers.

Ty Cobb may have been hotheaded, but he was also shrewd, calculating, and quick to take advantage of an enemy's weakness. In 1911, pursued by a youngster named Joe ("Shoeless Joe") Jackson, the Georgia Peach had to keep going at top speed all season. But at that, Jackson came into the last six games—they were against the Tigers—with an advantage of several points.

Realizing he had to do something to upset the rhythmic slugging of Jackson, Cobb employed a little psychology. He and Jackson were casual friends, but now Ty suddenly made a point of refusing to say one word to his opponent. He gave him the silent treatment. Jackson, a simple, uncomplicated youth, wondered what he had done to offend his erstwhile friend. While he was worrying, his batting fell off, and Cobb stepped out and won the batting title. His last-minute spurt sent his average zooming to a terrific .420.

Cobb battled right along, year after year. And year after year, he pulled the fans into ball parks all over the league. He was in the bigger money now, too. Cobb was astute enough to know his own value, and he made the Detroit management pay accordingly. Every year he held out for a raise, eventually boosting his salary to $40,000 a year.

Things were always happening to Cobb and his fellow Tigers in those days. There was the famous players' strike in 1912. It all began in New York, where a leather-lunged fan led a whole section of the stands in hurling abuse at the hated Cobb. Their remarks became so violent that Cobb lost his temper completely. He vaulted into the seats and handed out a savage beating to the noisy spectator. The latter deserved it, true, but Cobb was wrong in going into the stands. Ban Johnson, head of the American League, suspended him indefinitely.

The Detroit players had no particular love for Cobb, but they knew what he meant to their pennant chances. They held a meeting and decided to go on a strike unless he was reinstated. This was an unheard-of development. But those Tigers weren't fooling, and they refused to take the field against the Athletics in Philadelphia.

Now the Tiger management was in real trouble—it would cost them $5,000 if they couldn't put a team on the field. Manager Hughie Jennings, after scouring Philadelphia, finally came up with a group of semi-pros and schoolboys, put them in Detroit uniforms, and sent them out on the field. The game, of course, was a joke and the Athletics won as they pleased, 24–2. The angry Johnson threatened to throw every one of the Tigers out of baseball. Then Cobb himself stepped into the picture and urged the players to return to action. An agreement was finally reached: Ty's suspension was reduced to ten days, and the Tigers took the field in Washington.

Cobb batted and fought his way through the next few years. His string of batting titles was interrupted in 1916 when Tris Speaker, Cleveland's immortal center fielder, nosed him out. But Ty came right back to win in 1917, 1918, and 1919. His .384 in 1919 gave him his final batting championship. The following year (he was almost thirty-three years old then) he slipped to .334 and appeared in only 112 games. A damaged knee, the result of an outfield collision, had him on the bench for several weeks.

In 1921 Cobb succeeded Hughie Jennings as manager of the Tigers. He had great success in developing hitters, but his team lacked pitching strength. Despite the fact that Cobb had them fighting all the way, the Tigers came home in sixth place. Ty personally slammed the ball at a .389 pace, but it wasn't enough to regain his batting title. He was beaten out by a fellow Tiger, Harry Heilmann, who hit .394.

The next year Ty brought the Tigers up to third place, and in spite of his managerial worries he hit .401—the third time he reached the magic numbers. This time it was George Sisler, of the St. Louis Browns, who outdistanced the Georgia Peach, with .420.

For the next few years Ty struggled to bring home a pennant for the Detroit fans, but he never quite succeeded. He tried hard, and always told his men just what to do on every play. Once Bobby Veach was on first and Cobb was the next hitter. Before taking his place in the batter's box he rushed down to first to give Veach his instructions. Then he went back to the plate, bunted, and beat the throw to first base.

He called time again and trotted down to second to tell Veach what to do; then back to the plate to give the next hitter his orders. Finally play was resumed, and the batter hit into a double play, retiring the side. Veach intercepted Cobb on his way to the outfield. Breathlessly he asked, "What do I do now, Ty?"

In 1926, Cobb was his usual fighting self; he also knocked in runs, hit .339, and kept on stealing bases. But his individual efforts were not nearly enough and the Detroit club slipped into sixth place. That was the end of Cobb the manager, and at the close of the season, after twenty-two years of service to one club, he obtained his release.

Over in Philadelphia, Connie Mack heard the news and put in a bid for the old Tiger. Connie felt sure there was a year or two of good baseball left in Cobb—and he was right. In 1927, Cobb roamed the Philadelphia outfield in 134 games, hit a resounding .357—and lost an argument with an umpire. Against the Boston Red Sox in May he slammed a pitch over Shibe Park's right-field wall close to the foul line. The umpire called it foul and Ty complained too bitterly; he was fined and suspended for a brief period. The same old Cobb, even if he was in a new uniform!

In 1928, he helped spark the A's to a sensational rally in the late part of the season. The drive fell short, but Ty and his new teammates had given the Yankees a bad scare. At the end of that season Ty decided to call it a career—and it was surely the finest in the annals of the game. Small wonder that he was the first star to be named for the Cooperstown Hall of Fame in 1936.

Ty retired to a life of luxury, for he was as shrewd with his financial investments as he had been on the baseball field. He became very wealthy. In fact, his fortune was estimated in 1947 at approximately $7,000,000.

He must have missed the smoke of battle. Certainly the game missed him. On September 27, 1947, Ty and a collection of other former baseball greats returned to Yankee Stadium for "Old Timers' Day." The aging stars climbed into uniforms and played a two-inning game for fun. Cobb got a tremendous round of applause from a new generation of fans when he stepped up to the plate. Still keen of eye, the sixty-one-year-old batting king laid down a fine bunt and trundled off to first. Twenty years before he would have been safe—or he would have given the umpire a bitter argument. But that day he just grinned and trotted back to the bench. The Peach didn't have to worry about base hits any more. He could sit back and watch the younger men make their futile attacks on his records.

He'll never be forgotten. The name of Ty Cobb will always symbolize the national game at its fiercest and most exciting. For Ty Cobb, more than any other athlete, played to win.

The One and Only: Babe Ruth

The baseball book that doesn't carry at least one chapter on Babe Ruth has yet to be written. There's a good reason for this. Ruth was the most colorful figure ever to appear on the American sports scene, and the object of an almost insane hero worship on the part of millions of men and boys throughout the country.

Everything the man did, he did in a big way. He hit a baseball farther than any man in the world; he made more money, and he got into more trouble. In 1925, after gorging himself on a record number of hot dogs and bottles of soda pop, he even had the world's biggest stomach ache. It all but killed him.

The Babe was a fabulous figure, a Paul Bunyan of baseball; and he established in the 1920's and in the early 1930's hitting records that have a good chance of standing as long as the national game is played. In his twenty-one years in the big leagues, he rapped out 730 home runs (including World Series and All-Star games), 60 of them in one season alone, and he had a lifetime batting average of .342. "Heck," he once said, "I coulda hit .600 if I had bothered with those little singles." But he knew that people came out to see him hit homers, and that's what he liked to do.

Babe Ruth didn't look like a champion athlete. He was built along the general lines of a barrel, with powerful arms and shoulders, a large torso, and thin, frail-looking legs. But he was a great natural ball player. He started out in an industrial school as a catcher, played first base, became the top southpaw pitcher in the American League, then settled down to a brilliant career as an outfielder. From the first day he came into the majors as a pitcher for the Boston Red Sox until that May 25, 1934, when he wound up his baseball life with three homers in one afternoon at Pittsburgh, he was Mr. Baseball. Legends grew up about him; men everywhere talked of his prodigious feats, his antics off the field, his colossal appetite, his love for kids.

Ruth's feats on the diamond were so spectacular that writers sometimes slipped into the realm of fantasy in reporting them. For instance, reams of colorful copy have been turned out to the effect that in the 1932 World Series (his last) Ruth pointed to a spot in the center-field stands where, he said, he was going to hit the next pitch. Then he did it. What actually happened was that Charlie Root, pitcher for the Chicago Cubs, got over a strike, and the Babe waved one finger. He waved two fingers after the next pitch to indicate two strikes—all the while keeping up a noisy conversation with Root, the Cub infield, and the Cub bench. Then he waved one finger straight at Root, yelling something like, "I still have one left!" He then walloped the next pitch into the far reaches of center field—giving birth to a legend which was, after all, only a bit of embroidery tacked on to an indisputable Ruthian feat of arms.

Although the Babe was a supershowman on the field, off it he was just a big, friendly guy who loved a good time. An absolute extrovert, he liked all kinds of people and especially boys. He never for a second forgot his own youth and the hard, hungry days on the streets of Baltimore.

The Babe did a lot for baseball. In the first place, his phenomenal feats helped the fans forget the Black Sox scandal of 1919, when members of the Chicago White Sox were found to have sold out the World Series to the Cincinnati Reds. In the second place, he changed the whole concept of the game. Teams stopped playing for just one run, went all out for the big inning that would send five or six runs across the plate. As a result of this, people who didn't know a squeeze play from a foul ball started fighting their way into ball parks just to see someone—preferably Ruth himself—hammer one over the fence. He brought the game down to a level where every man, woman, and child in the United States could get a thrill. In other words, he made the sport what it is today—our national game.

Baseball players themselves owe him a vote of thanks, too. His famous contract for $80,000 a year boosted salaries all over both leagues. A second-rate Chicago infielder would claim he was worth at least a fraction of that amount. He'd get it.

Babe Ruth was a tonic for the whole sport. But the game did a lot for him, too. It took a tough, half-wild, half-educated boy off those city streets and made him a wealthy, famous, and respected man.

Millions of words have been written about Ruth, and his story has been told again and again. One spring, fourteen years after he had played his last game, three books detailing his meteoric career appeared on the market. His fame will probably last for all time.

At the height of the Babe's career in the 1920's, all good Philadelphians hated and feared the powerful New York Yankees. And the man they hated and feared most was, of course, Ruth himself. How they dreaded to see him come up to the plate, particularly with men on base! And the Athletic pitcher who managed to retire him became a hero—at least temporarily.

He belted many a pitch over the right-field wall at Shibe Park. He would set himself in the box, wave his big bat slowly back and forth, then coil his whole body like a spring and bash the ball with everything he had. Sometimes he'd miss and even fall down from the force of his swing. But too often, for the Athletic fans, he would connect and send one of those high, long drives out to right field. Once he hit pitcher Lefty Grove for homers in successive times at bat, and the second of those drives not only cleared the fence but sailed over a row of houses that ran parallel to the wall. It was a colossal belt. Another day, another game, Ruth plastered a high drive toward dead center. The A's had just installed a new public-address system with a horn-shaped loudspeaker on top of the scoreboard, and the Babe's ball went right into the horn.

There was another time when he ruined what looked like a perfectly good Philadelphia victory by whacking out home runs in the seventh and eighth innings, each time with two men on base. The A's, who had been leading, 3–2, were finally walloped, 8–3. No wonder Philadelphians were afraid of him.

Babe Ruth inspired fear and amazement throughout the league. But even when he was wrecking their team, fans had to admire those hits of his. They were so high and so far that there was never any doubt about their leaving the park. They were complete and in themselves perfect. Babe Ruth hitting a homer was something to see.

No boy ever got off to a worse start in life than did George Herman Ruth. He was born February 6, 1895, in Baltimore, and first came to attention when he turned up in St. Mary's Industrial School at the age of seven. For many years, Ruth had little or nothing to say about his life prior to St. Mary's. It's enough to remark that it was cold and rough.

The good brothers at St. Mary's set out to teach the boy to be a tailor. Perhaps he would have been a good one—if he hadn't walked onto a baseball diamond. The game was made to order for him.

The youngster started out as a catcher, but was shifted to the pitching mound because of a shortage of hurlers. He was a standout immediately. One day, Jack Dunn, owner of the Baltimore Orioles, came out to watch him in action. He saw Ruth pitch a smooth game and help his own cause with two drives over the fence. That was enough for Dunn, who quickly signed up the young southpaw. Ruth was nineteen.

He pitched his first game of professional ball on April 22, 1914. Nervous at first, he settled down to win a 6–0 shutout. He pitched a few more games for Baltimore, and then was sold to the Boston Red Sox with two other players for $22,500.

For five years he was one of the best pitchers in the league. He once fanned the "murderers' row" of that day—Ty Cobb, Bobby Veach, and Sam Crawford—

with the bases full. He pitched the Red Sox to three American League pennants, and he set a World Series record with 29 consecutive scoreless innings. This record wasn't broken until 1961 when Whitey Ford of the Yankees completed 32 innings of scoreless World Series pitching.

In the 1916 Boston-Brooklyn set-to, Ruth started the second game. He gave up a home run in the first inning, then pitched thirteen blank frames and finally won, 2–1, in the fourteenth. In the 1918 Series he worked the first game against Jim Vaughan, of the Cubs, and turned in a sharp 1–0 victory. He was back again in the fourth game and went seven innings before the Cubs found him for two runs to tie the score at 2–2. Ruth was taken out of the box and shifted into the outfield so that the club could still have the advantage of his potent bat. Joe Bush went in to pitch the remaining innings, and the Sox won the game, 3–2. Winning pitcher: Babe Ruth.

The Babe was a great hurler. There was only one trouble: he was hitting too many homers. The Red Sox management concluded that it was to Boston's advantage to have that power in the line-up every day. So, in 1919, Ruth pitched only occasionally and was a regular in the outfield. He immediately broke the home-run record with the then outlandish total of 29 four-base blows. That was nothing to what the Babe had in store for the record books in the years to come.

About this time, however, owner Harry Frazee of

the Red Sox was beginning to realize he had too many irons in the fire. He was in serious financial trouble as a result of backing a couple of Broadway shows which turned out to be anything but hits. He solved his problem by selling Babe Ruth to the Yankees for something more than $100,000.

This developed into a great move for Ruth and the Yankees—they both prospered mightily. The Babe's debut in a New York uniform, however, was not too auspicious. It was on April 14, 1920, and Ruth contrived to drop a fly in the eighth inning, which gave the Athletics two runs and the game, 3–1. But he soon found the batting range in New York and broke his home-run record with a resounding 54. He batted at a sizzling .376; and the next year his home-run production zoomed to 59.

He was a big hit in New York. He was made for the Big Town, and it, he thought, was made for him. He lived accordingly. Training rules meant nothing. He could stay up all night, take a cold shower, then trot out on the field and win games for the Yankees. No ordinary mortal could keep pace with him, and several promising rookies who tried it quickly returned to the minors.

He lived a fast life, to put it mildly, and it's a wonder he survived. Once after a game in Washington, he and a few friends motored to Philadelphia. The Babe was at the wheel and, as usual, driving like the wind. Just outside the Quaker City, they crashed into a culvert. The car was wrecked and word somehow got around that Ruth had been killed. Actually, nobody was badly hurt, and Ruth appeared in right field the next day. He rapped out a homer, just to show that all was well.

His slugging startled the baseball world. In almost every American League city, he hit at least one homer that was the longest on record. In Detroit, he belted a ball that was said to have traveled 590 feet. In an exhibition game he hit an incredible 600-footer.

The 1922 Spalding Official Baseball Guide, discussing the 1921 season, under the appropriate subhead "Hits of Great Force" said: "Ruth played at Cincinnati in an exhibition game and batted the ball over the center-field fence and also into the right-field stands. That had never been done before. . . . In New York City Ruth twice batted a home run into the bleachers in center field. Baseball enthusiasts had gone to the Polo Grounds year after year awaiting the day when such a thing might happen, but most of them had given it up as an impossibility. Ruth twice convinced them it was not. . . . What better proof that this player is an athlete superior to all of his kind?"

The Yankees of that era were a wild, brawling crew, and Ruth was the ringleader. They caroused, fought among themselves, and all but drove manager Miller Huggins insane. Still, they kept on winning ball games. Ruth and Wally Pipp once slugged it out in the dugout in St. Louis and then went out and hit consecutive home runs. What could you do with a team like that? Huggins didn't know. Ruth got in at four o'clock one morning, and the little manager was all set to hand him a verbal blast and a stiff fine. But the Babe cannily stayed out of his way until game time, then slammed three homers to win for the Yanks.

There was one American League pitcher who thought he had the Ruth problem solved for a while. He was Hub Pruett, a young southpaw with the St. Louis Browns, who were fighting the Yankees for the pennant. Pruett had a snaky curve that broke away from the batter, and he fanned the Babe eleven out of the first thirteen times he faced him. He actually made Ruth look silly. Later on in the season, however, he abandoned the curve, threw Ruth a fast ball, and the Babe knocked it out of the park.

Ruth unaccountably came a cropper in the 1922 World Series. Nineteen times he stepped up to the plate against Giant pitchers, and he got just two hits and two bases on balls, for an average of .118. What was the answer? The Reach Guide was prompted to remark editorially that the Giants' smart pitchers had his number, that he could be stopped with low pitches and a change of pace. "Can Ruth come back?" asked the Guide. That was exactly five years before he achieved his record of 60 homers.

In 1923, the New York American League club opened Yankee Stadium. Sportswriters called it "the House That Ruth Built," and certainly the Babe had a lot to do with popularizing the Yankees. Some

60,000 fans crowded the new ball park that first day, and saw Ruth hit a homer with two on to beat the Red Sox, 4–1.

The Yanks were never checked for the rest of the season and won the pennant by seventeen games. They kept right on going through the World Series, finally beating McGraw's Giants, four games to two. Ruth, back in form again, took full revenge, banging Giant pitching for three home runs, a triple, a double, and two singles.

After leading the league with .378 in 1924, the Babe had one of his poorest years in 1925. It all started with a stomach ache, echoes of which were heard around the country. The Yanks were coming north at the close of their spring training, and when the train stopped at a little southern town to take on water, the Babe hopped off to take on refreshments. He is said to have gobbled up a dozen or so hot dogs with as many bottles of soda pop.

He was taken violently ill and rushed to a hospital in New York, where daily bulletins were issued to the anxious fans. It looked for a while as though he might even die. But his iron constitution pulled him through, and a month or so later he returned to the Yankee line-up. The Babe never got into his stride that year, however, and his constant warfare with Miller Huggins finally came to a head in St. Louis. His patience at last exhausted, the manager suspended him for thirty days and fined him $5,000.

Ruth roared back to New York, howling with rage. He probably didn't mind the fine, although it was the biggest ever levied on any player, as much as not being allowed to play baseball for a whole month. He rushed into owner Jake Ruppert's office and poured out his story. But Ruppert was no fool. He knew what Huggins was up against, and he made the fine and suspension stick. Furthermore, he talked Ruth into behaving himself—for a while, at least.

The next three years saw Babe Ruth at the peak of his game. And he could really play that game. He covered plenty of ground in right field, was fast on his feet, and had a wonderful throwing arm. And, of course, he slugged the ball as it had never been slugged before. He hit 47 homers in 1926 as the Yankees nosed out the Cleveland Indians for the American League pennant. They dropped the World Series to the St. Louis Cardinals, but the Babe walloped three homers in the fourth game, which the Yanks won, 10–5. He also had the dubious honor of ending the Series. He tried to steal second and was thrown out.

The 1927 Yankees were a superteam. They crushed the whole league, and the Babe, putting on a terrific spurt, cracked out 17 home runs in September to wind up with a total of 60 for the season, a record that wasn't topped until 1961 when Roger Maris electrified the baseball world with 61.

Babe Ruth was the biggest thing in sports now, and

he signed a contract calling for $80,000 a season. This was an incredible sum of money in those days, but undoubtedly he was worth it.

Although he now lived in luxury, he never forgot the youngsters. He was always ready to visit them in hospitals, sign autographs, and chat about the game they both loved. They seemed to understand each other, Ruth and the youngsters. Probably the most famous item in the Ruth legend concerns young Johnny Sylvester, who was ill in a hospital. Ruth went to see him, gave him an autographed baseball, and promised to hit a homer for him the next afternoon.

He hit the homer all right, and a few weeks later Johnny's father dropped around to Yankee Stadium, shook hands with the Babe, and thanked him for visiting the boy. "Johnny's doing fine now," he said.

"That's great!" boomed the Babe. Later he asked a teammate, "Who the heck is Johnny?"

He never could remember names, but it didn't worry him much. He called almost everybody "Kid." Young women he called "Sister." If they were over thirty-five, he called them "Mom."

Ruth's greatest World Series performance came in 1928 when the Yankees, after nosing out the Philadelphia Athletics in a torrid fight, scrambled the Cardinals in four straight games. It was a walkover, with not even a close score, and Ruth batted .625 and homered three times.

Although he was famous for home runs, one of the most memorable hits Ruth ever made went for only one base. It came in the last half of the ninth inning of a game in which the Yanks trailed by one run. They filled the bases and up came the Babe, with the crowd naturally screaming for a home run. Ruth took his usual stance at the plate, then just poked the ball into left field for a single. It caught the defense flat-footed, sent two runs across the plate, and won the game for New York. The Babe chuckled to himself as he trotted down to first base.

As the years rolled along, Ruth began to settle down. His forays into the night clubs became less frequent. He married Claire Hodgson in 1929 and spent more of his time with his family. There were two daughters: Julia, Claire's child by a previous marriage, and Dorothy, whom they adopted.

But out on the field he was the same old Babe, and it wasn't until 1933 that he started to show signs of slipping. He realized definitely the following season that his best years were behind him. He played only spasmodically, and was frequently relieved in the late innings. As with most great athletes, it was his legs that finally failed him.

He had been in the majors for two decades now, and more and more he thought of retiring to a managerial position. Naturally, he wanted to manage the Yankees, but Ruppert, although he recognized the Babe's greatness as a player, did not feel he was ready to take over the Yanks. He offered Ruth the job of managing Newark, a New York farm club in the International League.

Ruth, in a huff, turned it down. He asked for and got his unconditional release, and went to the Boston Braves as a coach and outfielder. It was sad. It was the end of an era.

But he made one last great gesture. He started the season for the Braves, and on May 25 in Pittsburgh he hit three gorgeous home runs. But that was the end; he couldn't stand the grind any longer. He quit a few days later.

Ruth lived quietly in New York for the next three years, then popped out of retirement briefly as a coach for the Brooklyn Dodgers in 1938. He couldn't get along with the management, however, so he soon abandoned that job.

The fact that he was independently wealthy meant little to the Babe. Throughout his life he had two main interests: baseball and kids. Now, in his later years, he still kept his contacts with the game, and worked hard to organize boys' baseball leagues. But he was unable to work as hard as he would have liked. His health was failing. Organized baseball honored him with a "day" on April 27, 1947, and he looked weak and tired as he acknowledged the cheers of thousands of fans at Yankee Stadium. In a hoarse voice that could hardly be heard and which brought tears to the eyes of those who remembered him in his lusty, younger days, the Babe said, "The only real game in the world is baseball."

The Babe was a sick man. He didn't know it, but he had cancer of the throat. He died August 16, 1948, and his body, lying in state in Yankee Stadium, was viewed by an estimated 100,000 persons.

All baseball fans felt they knew Babe Ruth personally. He was that kind of a man. He was the greatest single figure in the history of sports.

Saga of a Rajah: Rogers Hornsby

The somewhat turbulent major-league career of Rogers Hornsby began with the St. Louis Cardinals in 1915 and ended with the St. Louis Browns in 1937. In the intervening twenty-two years, Rog firmly established himself as the greatest right-handed hitter in National League history.

He was also something of a stormy petrel; as a result, he was shuffled from one club to another and spent part of his baseball life a virtual exile in the minor leagues. Hornsby was a cold-eyed man who said exactly what he thought, and didn't care who

SAGA OF A RAJAH

was on the receiving end of his remarks. He spoke his mind sharply, honestly—and perhaps tactlessly. Certain owners took a dim view of this, and that's one of the reasons Rog found himself in relative obscurity in Texas, managing a minor-league team, when he was finally voted into the Cooperstown Hall of Fame in 1942.

The thunder from Hornsby's bat echoed all over the league in the 1920's as he hammered his way to seven batting titles, six of them in succession. He set a modern National League record in 1924 when he slugged the ball for a sizzling .424. He once hit safely in 33 straight games, and although he was mainly a line-drive hitter, he led his league in home-run production in 1922 and 1925. Like most great players, he was at his best when the chips were down, when men were on the bases; twelve times during his career he stepped up to the plate with bases full and smashed the ball into the stands or over the fence. Altogether, "the Rajah" (as he was nicknamed) sent a total of 1,582 runs across the plate for five different major-league teams.

A story, possibly unauthentic but which at least conveys some idea of the power in Hornsby's bat, concerns Hornsby and Jake Fournier, first baseman for the Brooklyn Dodgers. One afternoon in 1923, the Cards were battling the Dodgers at Ebbets Field when Rog came up to bat in the first inning. A rookie was on the mound for Brooklyn, and he went into a huddle with the veteran Fournier.

"Pitch him on the inside," said Jake promptly.

The young hurler followed his advice, and Hornsby slammed a vicious double down the left-field line. The pitcher wheeled on Fournier with fire in his eye.

"That's all right," said Jake. "Keep 'em on the inside to Hornsby. I have a family to support. I don't want to get killed by one of those line drives!"

Rog had a smooth, easy, rhythmic swing, and it was a pleasure to watch him go to work on a pitcher, even when he was busy doing irreparable damage to your own team. Blessed with a great pair of eyes, he seldom swung at a bad pitch but waited until he got the one he wanted and then murdered it. He was a thoroughly competent fielder, too, but it was with his bat that he wrote his name in the record books.

Rogers Hornsby was born in Winters, Texas, on April 27, 1896. When he was still a baby the family moved to Fort Worth, where Rog grew up and went to school. He loved baseball from the first time he saw it played, and whenever he had a spare moment from his part-time job as messenger at the stockyards, he was out on the sandlots of Fort Worth. He was only fifteen years old when he joined a semi-pro team backed by a Mr. H. L. Warlick.

Warlick used the boy in twelve games and paid him at the rate of $2 a game. This wasn't much, but Rog was so crazy to play ball that he didn't care.

On the personal side, he was a lively youngster, aggressive and sure of himself. He must have been an impertinent one, too, for one day, coming back from a ball game, a veteran pitcher complimented him on his playing. "You did a fine job at second today," the pitcher said.

"Yeah," Hornsby agreed, "and there are eight other positions I can play just as well."

Rog was good and he knew it. The following year he got a tryout with a minor-league team, Dallas. He showed lots of promise but was still too green for such experienced company; he was sent to a less important team in the East Texas League and later to a team in the Texas-Oklahoma League. There was little that was extraordinary about his work in the minors—in fact, he never hit even .300 until he arrived in the big leagues.

A St. Louis scout, however, was impressed with his speed and aggressiveness, and, after spending most of the 1915 season with another minor-league team in the Western Association, Rog was brought up to the Cardinals. His salary had been $90 a month, and when he arrived in St. Louis he had $2.08. Nobody, with the possible exception of Hornsby himself, guessed that within a few years he would be a $40,000-a-year star.

He played his first game on September 10, and finished out the season at second for the Cardinals. The thin, long-legged boy with a world of pep soon made a regular place for himself on the team. In his second year, he played 129 games and hit a reasonable .313.

Up to this time, Rog had been choking the

bat—that is, holding it part way up the handle. With this grip he would try to poke the ball into the outfield. But now the Texan began to fill out, and almost overnight he became a powerfully built man. A coach, noting those big shoulders, suggested that he grip the bat at the end and get his weight into the swing. The result was that balls began to bounce off walls all over the league.

It was in 1920 that Hornsby, with a .370 mark, embarked on a reign of terror in which he lambasted National League pitching and won the batting crown for half a dozen years in succession. The next season he hit .397, the highest National League average in twenty-one years, and the New York Giants offered $250,000 for his services. Not a chance, said St. Louis owner Sam Breadon.

The Cardinals of the '20's could hit like fiends, but they were woefully short on pitchers. In one game against the Boston Braves, the Card batting order exploded for ten straight hits in one inning. They won that game all right, but in the main they couldn't overcome the lack of hurling strength; they finished fifth in the league in 1920, third in 1921.

The second baseman from Texas really hit the jackpot in 1922, and on the strength of his phenomenal slugging the St. Louis team battled in the first division most of the year. On June 29 at Pittsburgh, Hornsby hit his sixteenth homer; it was a long, whistling liner between the scoreboard and the right-field bleachers. This was the first time a ball had been hit so far at Forbes Field. On July 28, his twenty-seventh homer against the Giants tied the old National League record, and a few days later No. 28 against the Philadelphia Phillies broke the record. He got fourteen more before the season was over.

He maintained his savage pace right down to the end. Three hits in five times at bat on the last day sent his average to .401, the highest National League batting mark in twenty-three years.

Although the gangling rookie had developed into a great star, he didn't let it go to his head. On the field, he was still driving and fighting for every ball game. Off the field, he lived quietly with his family. If he had a weakness, it was for steaks. They say he never missed a chance to check up on the best steak house in every city the Cardinals visited.

During the 1923 season, there was a flurry of trouble between St. Louis manager Branch Rickey and his star second baseman. After a particularly noisy verbal clash, Rog was fined and briefly suspended. He played in only 107 games, but he hit .384 and was again the National League's batting king.

The Cardinals fell to sixth place in 1924, but Hornsby was the terror of the league. He set a modern National League record with a terrific .424 average, as he led the pack for the fifth consecutive year. He was the most feared batter in baseball, and rival managers grew prematurely gray trying to figure out ways of stopping the Rajah. None of their schemes worked, and the big Texan rapped out 227 hits for 373 total bases. It was the greatest burst of hitting the National League had ever seen. Yet he lost the Most Valuable Player award because one writer felt he wasn't as good a team player as Dazzy Vance, the Brooklyn right-hander who won twenty-eight games while losing only six. What does a man have to do? Rog must have wondered.

Wealthier clubs continued to angle for the great second sacker. This time it was Phil Wrigley, owner of the Chicago Cubs, who offered a fabulous sum for him; but again the Cardinal office said no—they had bigger plans for Hornsby.

Midway through May of 1925, it was obvious that a shake-up was coming in St. Louis. The Cards had gotten off to a slow start, and Sam Breadon decided he had had enough of manager Branch Rickey. It was time for a change.

The new manager, to the surprise of practically no one, was Rogers Hornsby. In addition to becoming head man on the field, he also acquired Rickey's Cardinal stock for some $50,000. This turned out to be a very profitable negotiation for the Texan.

With Hornsby barking the orders and setting a graphic example of how the game should be played, the rejuvenated Cardinals swept up from the cellar and finished in fourth place. Rog, despite his new responsibilities, rapped out 39 homers and rattled the fences for a .403 average to lead the league for the sixth straight year. The authoritative Reach Baseball Guide went all out in its praise of the slugger and called him "the mightiest hitter of all time." It wasn't far from being right.

As a manager, Rogers hit his peak in 1926. At the beginning of the spring-training sessions, he announced confidently and grimly to his squad that this was the year the Cardinals were going to win. There were troublesome times ahead, but he never wavered from his original prediction.

It was Hornsby who insisted on the purchase of Grover Cleveland Alexander, and the veteran right-hander made Hornsby smile with his consistent and heady pitching. During the last week in August, the Cards met the Pittsburgh Pirates in a crucial six-game series. It was freely predicted that this set of games would decide the championship of the league.

Thanks to the heroic work of Alexander and Jess Haines, the Cardinals broke out of the series with four victories and one tie, and a hold on first place. Once in the lead, there was no stopping them. Their eastern trip was the clincher. They trimmed the Phillies five out of six games; one of their victories was a 23–3 walloping in which the whole murderous line-up took part in slamming hits off the walls of old Baker Bowl. On September 24, the St. Louis battering ram seized the pennant with a 6–4 victory at the Polo Grounds in New York.

In his first full year as a manager Rogers Hornsby had brought home a winner, but his jubilation quickly turned to grief. A few days before the opening of the World Series, he received the sad news that his mother had died in Texas. He couldn't even attend the funeral, and his tight-lipped determination to stay with his team won him the sympathy and respect of fans all over the nation.

The Cardinals' foes in the championship games were the mighty New York Yankees, and Hornsby's team was not conceded much of a chance with the perennial American League winners. It was said that Babe Ruth, Lou Gehrig, Herb Pennock & Co. would be too much for the St. Louis entry.

Hornsby read the news stories and sneered. He knew his team and he told them bluntly, as he had told them in the spring, that there was no team, not even the Yankees, that could stand against them.

The Cards believed him. Although they got off on the wrong foot when Pennock shaded Willie Sherdel 2–1 in a brilliant southpaw pitching duel, they came back with a rush to win the second game, 6–2, behind the steady pitching of Alexander.

The scene shifted to St. Louis, and the Yankees knew they were in a fight when Jess Haines blanked them with five hits to give the Cardinals a 2–1 advantage.

Led by the one and only Babe Ruth, who slashed out three homers, the Yanks crushed the Cards, 10–5, in the fourth game. Hornsby wasn't worried; he figured to take the lead again with Sherdel in the next game. Willie turned in his second straight well-pitched game, but again Pennock turned in a better one, and the Yankees took the game, 3–2. Now the

Cardinals were in trouble. They had dropped two out of three on their own field and were faced with the necessity of winning two straight in Yankee Stadium.

Back in New York, Rog sent Alexander against the Yankees, and the Cardinal sluggers made it easy for "Old Pete." Hammering out thirteen hits, they trimmed the New Yorkers, 10–2, and tied the Series at three games apiece.

The pay-off game began under cloudy skies and developed into a pitching duel between Haines and Waite Hoyt. The Yankees broke through in the third inning when Ruth homered, but the Cards, alertly taking advantage of sloppy fielding by the New Yorkers, rushed three runs across the plate in the fourth. Although the Yanks scored in the sixth on a double and a single, the Cards clung doggedly to the lead.

Haines was beginning to show signs of wear and tear, however, and this brought about a dramatic incident in the last of the seventh inning. Earle Combs, representing the tying run, singled and was sacrificed to second. Cardinal strategy called for an intentional pass to Ruth; and when Bob Meusel, the next batter, forced the Bambino at second, Combs raced to third. Pitching to Lou Gehrig, Haines lost control and walked the hard-hitting first baseman to fill the bases.

Rog had to think fast now. The World Series was slipping from his grasp. Another pass would force in the tying run; any kind of hit would mean two runs and probably the game, since the Cardinal hitters had been stopped completely since the fourth inning.

Hornsby spoke briefly to Haines. Blood dripped from one of the pitcher's fingers—he had been working so hard with a curve that he had rubbed the skin off. No wonder he was losing control.

Rog took one look, patted Haines on the back, and waved toward the bull pen. In strode the nonchalant figure of Alexander. He was close to forty years old and he had pitched nine innings the day before, but he was ready to go again. Waiting for him at the plate was Tony Lazzeri, who had driven in more than 100 runs during the regular season.

Alexander took his time warming up, then whipped his first pitch in for a called strike. Every fan in the park jumped to his feet on the next pitch: Lazzeri rammed a savage liner into the stands—foul by a couple of feet. With the fans still on their feet, Lazzeri went down swinging on the third pitch. The Cards still led, 3–2.

That was the ball game. Alexander retired three Yankees in a row in the eighth, and the first two men in the ninth. Then up stepped Babe Ruth. Old Pete pitched carefully, refusing to give the great slugger anything that he might hit out of the park, and finally walked him. Then, with Meusel at the plate, Ruth, thinking to catch the Cardinals napping, broke for second. Catcher Bob O'Farrell snapped a peg to second base, and Hornsby himself tagged Ruth for the final out of the Series.

St. Louis was, to put it mildly, very much pleased with its first world championship, and no man stood higher than the brawny Texan who had led the team to victory. It was the high point of his career, even though he was but thirty years old.

Then came the blow. During the following winter Hornsby was involved in one of the most criticized deals in baseball history. St. Louis fans were outraged when, in December, Sam Breadon announced that he had traded Rogers to the New York Giants for Frankie Frisch and Pitcher Jimmy Ring. It was unbelievable. The man who had brought the city its first world title was being sent away almost immediately after achieving his triumph!

What was behind this bit of master-minding still remains something of a secret. It was no secret, however, that Rogers had quarreled with Breadon. The latter now saw a chance to rid himself of a problem and at the same time pick up another fine second baseman in Frisch. Whatever his reasons, Breadon let himself in for a lot of abuse from the fans and newspapers of the Mound City. He was bombarded with phone calls, letters, and telegrams. Eventually, of course, all the hullabaloo died down, and Frankie Frisch became a great favorite in St. Louis.

As for the businesslike Hornsby, he shrugged his shoulders and moved calmly into the camp of John McGraw, the famous manager of the Giants. But before leaving St. Louis, he had to dispose of his

Cardinal stock which he had originally obtained from Rickey. He sold the stock at a profit of some $70,000, which probably helped compensate for any pangs he may have felt at leaving St. Louis.

The record books will tell you that Rog had a great year with the Giants. He batted at a .361 clip, knocked out 26 homers, and generally conducted himself like one of the greatest infielders in the game, which he was. Nevertheless, he was on his way out before the season was over.

What happened? Well, the former undisputed leader of the World Champions now found himself in the position of having to take orders. McGraw was the boss here. He did, however, make Hornsby his field captain; and when he was ill, which happened several times, he put Rog in charge of the club. Rog had his own ideas about how baseball should be played. "McGraw does it this way," a player retorted in answer to criticism from Hornsby. "When McGraw's here, do it his way, but when I'm running things, you'll do it my way!" snarled Hornsby. This sort of talk didn't go too well with the New Yorkers. It may have been that Rog was too much of a perfectionist. He expected everybody to be able to play baseball the way he played it. Obviously, this wasn't fair—Hornsby was great. But his cold intolerance of the mistakes of others, plus a late-season run-in with owner Charley Stoneham, probably helped shorten his days in a New York uniform. So despite his heroic work with the third-place Giants, he was traded again at the end of the season. This time he went to the Boston Braves.

With the second-division Braves, Hornsby really went on the warpath. He again led the league as he pounded the ball for a terrific .387 and rammed out 21 homers. On May 23, he was named manager of the club, but—lacking the necessary material—he was unable to bring the team any higher than seventh place. He was on his way again at the end of the season, to the Chicago Cubs this time, in exchange for five players and $120,000.

Cub fans were delighted with the acquisition of the great Hornsby and immediately started talking about a pennant. The 1929 Cubs were a sound team, with such hitters as Woody English, Hack Wilson, and Kiki Cuyler, and hurling strength in Charlie Root, Guy Bush, and Pat Malone, among others.

The Rajah fitted in well with this collection of stars, and his big bat sparked the team to a National League championship. All Rog did was wallop the ball for a neat .380 and crash out 40 home runs as the Cubs charged into a World Series with the power-laden Philadelphia Athletics.

Here the Cubs were overmatched. Connie Mack's pitchers worked carefully on Rog and held him to five hits during the Series. The only time he was able to do any damage was in the third game, when he furnished most of the punch with a double and a base hit that led to the Cubs' single victory in the Series. The Athletics were overpowering in the remaining games.

The Cubs were not disgraced in losing to one of the finest teams in history.

It wasn't long before Hornsby was a manager again. When Joe McCarthy stepped down in September of 1930, Rog took over and drove the Cubs into second place, only two games behind the Cardinals.

His batting fell off slightly in 1931, as well it might after sixteen years. Nevertheless, one afternoon in April he showed there was still plenty of punch left when he rapped out three homers in successive times at bat.

Trouble plagued him the following year when he became involved in a legal dispute with a gambler. In what appeared to be an attempt to ruin his career, a bookmaker sued him for some $50,000. The case was thrown out of court, but the damage had been done, and Hornsby was through in Chicago. On August 2, Charlie Grimm became manager.

Somehow, Hornsby caught on again with the Cardinals as a part-time second baseman and pinch hitter. He got into 46 games and delivered enough base blows to make up a .325 batting average. In July of 1933, he got an offer from the St. Louis Browns of the American League. They needed a manager, and the Cardinals released Rog so he could take the job.

The Browns of those days were a rather hopeless outfit. There was no money for players, and few people seemed to care where the team finished. Rog gave the job everything he had, but he couldn't drag the Browns out of the second division. He made no attempt to play regularly, but confined his activities to an occasional few innings at second or swinging a pinch hitter's bat.

Eventually, he disagreed with owner Donald Barnes and left St. Louis again. The next few years found him in a variety of jobs: coach with the Baltimore Orioles; manager of Chattanooga, manager of the Orioles, then of Oklahoma, of Fort Worth; later a sports broadcaster, and finally a newspaperman. He also ran an annual baseball school for boys. A hundred or so ambitious youngsters attended these schools each spring, and some of them were started on their way to the major leagues.

Rog was with Fort Worth in 1942 when he was elected to the Hall of Fame. It is ironical that this man, who had been a wonderful player and a successful manager when he had the material, should, for whatever reason, have found himself deep in the minor leagues at the time this honor was given to him.

He was destined to get another chance, however. After several successful seasons managing in the minors, he was brought back to the big leagues and took over the St. Louis Browns. But he was far too serious about the game to get along with the lighthearted owner, Bill Veeck. That arrangement was terminated in midseason of 1952. Rog caught on again as head man of the Cincinnati Reds and did a good job with a mediocre team. But again, differences with the front office caused his dismissal. It was getting to be an old story—and not a very happy one.

Although he had trouble with owners, Hornsby could teach baseball, and he improved batting averages wherever he went. The sports world was saddened in January, 1963, when the slugger underwent eye surgery and shortly thereafter suffered a stroke, from which he never recovered. He was sixty-six. When he died, the game lost a great one.

Connie's Kids: Al Simmons and Mickey Cochrane

Connie Mack, the "Grand Old Man of Baseball" who managed the Philadelphia Athletics for a fantastic fifty-seven years, started building his last great baseball machine in the early 1920's. This was the fine club that tore the American League apart and made off with two world titles. And two of the outstanding stars who made that team go were Al Simmons and Mickey Cochrane.

The slugging outfielder and the fiery catcher made many a summer afternoon unbearable for American League pitchers. They were Connie Mack's pride and joy, and he never seemed to tire of talking about them.

Perhaps Cochrane was his favorite. Of all the men who came and went during his half-century with the A's, probably none stood higher with Mack than the black-haired boy from Bridgewater, Massachusetts. But Simmons, the great slugger and fierce competitor from Milwaukee, made the old man's eyes light with joy as he blasted out his long hits, so many of them coming in crucial late-inning spots.

Al Simmons was a scrapper. He had to be, for things never came very easily for him. He was born May 22, 1903, the son of John and Agnes Szymanski. Aloysius Harry was one of a large family—he had three brothers and three sisters—and there was never too much of anything for anybody.

He went to public school in Milwaukee until he was fourteen. Then, to help out the family, he took a job in a shoe factory at $14 a week. Later he moved to the Wisconsin Motor Company, where he was paid the princely sum of $16 a week.

Al was sixteen and playing for semi-pro teams around Milwaukee when a scout for the Milwaukee Brewers, of the Triple A American Association, spotted the rangy youngster at the plate, noticed the ball bouncing off the wall, and signed him up.

"In those days," said Al, "I played all over the place. I wasn't much of a fielder, but I sure liked to hit that ball!"

Milwaukee farmed him out for two years, first to

Aberdeen, South Dakota, and then to Shreveport, Louisiana. He was still using his right name, but, the story goes, a Milwaukee sports reporter got tired of trying to keep the s's and z's straight and changed the name to Simmons. That was all right with Al—he didn't care how they spelled it.

Near the end of the 1923 season he was recalled to Milwaukee, where he played the last 20 games and hit .398. Connie Mack was impressed and bought him at a bargain-basement price.

At the Athletics' training camp in Fort Myers, Florida, the next spring, Al was almost lost in the shuffle. Everybody was watching Paul Strand, the most heralded rookie of the year. As it turned out, Strand, also an outfielder, failed to make the grade, while the unknown Simmons went on to become one of baseball's great hitters.

Al probably would have attracted even less attention if it hadn't been for his outlandish stance at the plate. He stood with his right foot far back and to the right—"one foot in the water bucket," sports writers said.

Simmons could never explain how he happened to develop that peculiar stance. "It just felt natural," he said. "Heck, I couldn't hit it any other way."

As for Connie Mack, he said, "My goodness, I don't care how he stands up there as long as he keeps on getting those hits."

Young Simmons was on his way; and although his first year was not sensational, it was completely adequate. Mack's new left fielder played 152 games, batted .308, and showed a definite tendency to hit a long ball. He was only twenty-one years old, however, and still had a lot to learn about playing the outfield in the big leagues.

"Mack was always waving a scorecard at me," he said, with a smile. "He moved me all around the field, and you know what? He was almost always right. Nine times out of ten the hitter would smack one right at me."

It was the following year—1925—that Al really hit his stride. The A's of that year were a colorful young team. In addition to Simmons there were Mickey Cochrane, Lefty Grove, Jimmy Dykes, Bing Miller, Eddie Rommel, and other firebrands. They made up a scrappy, noisy club—and they all but fought their way to a pennant.

They became known — and hated — around the league for their baiting tactics. "We had some great bench jockeys," Al said. "Cochrane was good. Rommel was another. I wasn't bad."

On June 15 the young A's put on one of the most sensational rallies in baseball history. They were taking a terrible beating from the Cleveland Indians at Shibe Park. After seven and a half innings, the score stood Cleveland 15, Philadelphia 4. Then it happened. Connie's batting order exploded, runs poured over the plate, Indian pitchers rushed in—and out.

Ten runs had come in and there were still two men on base, when Simmons came to bat. He had already hit safely once in the history-making inning. Now it was up to him to provide the finishing punch. The great young slugger, always at his best in a pinch, teed off on the third pitch and rammed a savage line drive into the stands in left field. That was all—but it was enough. Thirteen runs had come in, and the Philadelphia pitcher easily retired the groggy Indians in the top of the ninth. Final score: Philadelphia 17, Cleveland 15.

Through the next two months the Athletics, getting fine pitching from Sam Gray, Rommel, and Bryan ("Slim") Harriss, and heavy hitting from Simmons, Cochrane, and Miller, battled the World Champion Washington Senators for the league lead. Mack's team was exciting to watch—something was always happening at Shibe Park in those days.

On August 7, the A's lost the first game of a double-header with the Indians, and Eddie Rommel went looking for his nineteenth victory of the season in the nightcap. He quickly became entangled in a brilliant pitching duel with George Uhle, the Cleveland ace. In the last of the seventh, Mickey Cochrane singled to left center for the Athletics' first hit, and Simmons followed with the second and last hit. It was his eighteenth homer and accounted for the only two runs of the game. It was a tough loss for Uhle, but Rommel was the better pitcher that day, allowing only two singles. The game, played in the remarkable time of sixty-five minutes, established an American League record for brevity.

Simmons, having a big year for himself, once hit in 22 straight games before being stopped by Red Ruffing, then with the Red Sox. On August 18, Mack started his last western trip of the season, with his Athletics leading the league by two games. If he had known what was going to happen, he would have stayed at home in Philadelphia.

The team collapsed under the grueling strain of a tough pennant fight, dropped thirteen out of fifteen games, and was barely able to hold second place against the onrushing Browns. Though pennant hopes went up in smoke, Simmons kept right on hammering the ball and fighting for games. He wound up the season with a .386 batting average. Only Harry Heilmann with .393 and Tris Speaker with .389 topped Mack's great young outfielder. His 253 hits, more than any player in either league, included 24 home runs and went for a total of 392 bases.

Thus ended the Milwaukeean's first big season in the majors. He was destined to have many more, however, for he had arrived. In 1926 the A's fell to third place behind the Indians and Yankees, but Al hit .343. The next year Ty Cobb, Eddie Collins, and Zach Wheat joined the A's as Mack attempted to bolster his team with fading stars. It didn't work, but again Simmons slugged the ball viciously and wound up with a .392 average, again trailing Heilmann, with .398. The A's almost caught the Yanks in 1928, but a late-season double defeat in New York wrecked them. Their left fielder, however, continued to hit, and finished the season with a .351 average.

The year 1929 was a historic one in baseball, for it witnessed Philadelphia's first pennant in fourteen years.

The A's had a really terrifying batting punch that year. Simmons, young Jimmy Foxx, Cochrane, Mule Haas, and Miller hit hard and often. They started off fast and were leading the league by seven and a half games when they went into Yankee Stadium on June 21 for five games with the New Yorkers. A crowd of 70,000 came out for a double-header the first day, and they got their money's worth. They saw Lefty Grove, at his best, win the first game, 11–1. They saw their own Babe Ruth crack homers in the seventh and eighth innings, each with two men on base, to win the second game, 8–3. And they saw Al Simmons have one of the greatest days of his career. He crashed out eight hits in nine times at bat. Three singles and two homers whistled off his bat in the first game, and in the nightcap he was good for two doubles and a single. Eight hits, four of them for extra bases! He always considered that his top performance. Nonchalantly he would say, "I went eight for nine once at the Stadium."

The A's took two out of the next three from the Yanks, and never broke stride thereafter. They won the pennant by eighteen games. In left field Simmons stood head and shoulders over all other American League gardeners. Not only did he hit .365 and knock out 34 home runs, but he covered the field like a deer and had a fast and accurate arm.

The Chicago Cubs took the National League pennant in 1929, but they were no match for the Philadelphians in the World Series. Connie Mack got the jump when slow-baller Howard Ehmke, a surprise choice, won the first game, 3–1, and struck out thirteen Cubs in the process. Simmons failed to hit in his first World Series game, but he made up for it the next day. With a home run and a single, he knocked in four runs as the A's made it two straight by winning 9–3.

That homer came in the eighth inning, and it showed the power the young Pole was getting into his swing. With Cochrane on first, the Cub catcher figured the hit-and-run was on and called for a pitch-out. The ball was way outside, but Simmons stepped into it anyway and knocked it into the right-field stands.

When the World Series shifted to Philadelphia, Guy Bush gave the Cubs a temporary lift as he stopped the A's, 3–1, for Chicago's only victory.

That set the stage for one of the most dramatic innings in baseball history. The fourth game started quietly; there was no scoring in the first three innings. Then the Cubs went to work and piled up an 8–0 lead.

In the dugout Mack was disgusted. "If they don't wake up," he told one of his coaches, "I'll take them out and put in the rookies."

Al must have heard him. He led off in the last of the seventh and put one of Charlie Root's best pitches on top of the left-field stands for a homer. All that accomplished apparently was to rob Root of a shutout. But when Foxx, Miller, and Jimmy Dykes singled in succession for another run, the crowd woke up, and Mack thought he might leave the regulars in. Joe Boley and Max Bishop drilled two more singles, scoring the third and fourth runs of the inning. The Cubs started changing pitchers, but the A's continued hitting. Mule Haas belted an inside-the-park home run, scoring three more, and the big Chicago lead was reduced to one run. Cochrane walked, and Simmons came up for the second time. He singled to center on the three-and-one pitch, and Cochrane moved to second. When big Jimmy Foxx rammed his second hit of the inning, Mickey tore in from second with the tying run and Simmons galloped to third. Pat Malone came in to pitch for the Cubs, and the first thing he did was to pass Miller and load the bases. Jimmy Dykes, never a great hitter, came through in fine style. He banged a double to left, and Simmons and Foxx crossed the plate with the ninth and tenth runs of the inning. That ended the fireworks, but it was enough to set a World Series record and demoralize the Cubs. Lefty Grove held the 10–8 lead, fanning four of the six Cubs he faced in the last two innings.

There was one big moment left in the World Series of 1929. That came in the ninth inning of the next game. Again the A's were behind, this time by 2–0. With one out, Bishop shot a single over third base, and then the vast crowd went wild as Haas hit the first pitched ball over the right-field wall, tying the score at 2–2.

"It looked like extra innings when Cochrane rolled out to Hornsby," Simmons later said. "But I was lucky and got hold of a fast ball and knocked it up against the scoreboard for two bases. Boy, I was sure excited then. There I was down on second with the run that would give us the World Series—if I could just get in with it.

"Well, Foxx was up next and the pitcher decided to pass him and take a chance on Miller. Bing nailed one; and with two gone, I lit out for home as fast as I could go. Heck, I could've walked in. That ball hit the scoreboard, too, only I didn't know it then. Everybody was yelling and screaming and I just kept running. When I got home, it was all over. Boy, what a day that was!"

The man from Milwaukee was at the top now, a big star with a World Champion aggregation. But more honors and bigger days were coming up.

The 1930 Philadelphia machine didn't function very well in the early part of the season and ran into difficulty with the Washington Senators. In fact the Washington club was in first place by four and a half games when it came to Philadelphia for two games on Memorial Day.

That was another memorable occasion for Al Simmons. In the morning game the A's trailed the high-riding Senators, 6–3, as they came to the last half of the ninth. Spencer Harris singled to right. Bishop and Haas were retired, but a pinch hitter, Dib Williams, kept the game alive with a single to left.

Up to the plate came Simmons, and he was in no mood to be trifled with. He had been set down on three previous attempts, the fans were riding him, and his own teammates were kidding him.

"Think that guy'll ever get another hit?" Dykes said in a loud voice to Haas.

"Maybe—next year," Mule answered in equally loud tones.

Simmons heard them, all right, and he burned—even though he had been around long enough to know that every batter occasionally goes into a slump.

"Oh, they're all easy," he used to say, "when you're going good. But when you're not, even a schoolboy can get you out."

Washington's Ad Liska was no schoolboy, but he didn't get Al out either. Standing up there, growling at himself, at the pitcher, and at the world in general, the big slugger wanted nothing so much as a base hit. And he got it. He took out his bad temper on the third pitch and slammed it into the stands for a game-tying homer.

That, of course, fixed everything. The fans were with him to a man, his mates crowded around to slap him on the back, and he himself was in his usual good humor.

The game rattled on into extra innings. Al singled in the eleventh but didn't score. In the thirteenth he doubled to left center. Then came what might have been a serious accident. Foxx got an infield hit to the right side, and Al tore around third, saw he couldn't make home, and tried to scramble back. Caught in a run-down, he finally dove for the bag and made it safely. But that sudden twist had done something to his knee—he could hardly stand. A minute later when Eric McNair hit cleanly to center, Al was barely able to limp across with the winning run.

Immediately the club doctor, Mack, and players swarmed around. They discovered he had broken a blood vessel.

"He'll have to rest," said the physician.

"All right," said Mack, "but let him rest on the bench. Maybe I can use him as a pinch hitter."

George Earnshaw started the second game for the A's, and again the Senators piled up a lead. It was 7–4 in the seventh and the A's had two men on, when Al got the nod from Connie.

"If I hit it, I'll have to walk around," Al said. And, of course, that's what happened. He hit another home run in the clutch, and the A's went on to win, 14–11. As for Al, he went to the hospital for a few days.

Clark Griffith, veteran owner of the Senators, said

Simmons alone wrecked the chances of his 1930 team. "That fellow hit fourteen home runs in the eighth and ninth innings," Griffith said, "and every one of them figured in winning a game for Mack." The Athletics clinched their second straight pennant in Chicago on September 19. Simmons hit .381 and was American League batting champion. He was also a hard man to get out in the World Series, which the A's won from the St. Louis Cardinals, four games to two. Al hit .364, knocking out home runs in the first and last games. Hero of the classic, however, was big George Earnshaw, who pitched three brilliant games.

Al Simmons had his last really top year in 1931. Once again he was the champion batter with a mark of .390. Again he was the most feared clutch hitter in baseball, and again he led the Athletics to a pennant, their third straight.

Although he batted eight runs across the plate in the World Series, the Cardinals upended the A's, four games to three, and ended the domination of the Philadelphians.

But the real crack-up of the team came in 1932. Although they did manage to win 94 games, they couldn't even make it close for the Yankees. Simmons fell to .322, his lowest average since joining the A's eight years before. He was somewhat overshadowed by his teammate Jimmy Foxx, who batted a strong .364 and racked up 58 homers, only two short of Babe Ruth's record 60.

Al didn't know it, but he was through in Philadelphia. Mack didn't want to let him go, but a depression was in full swing and Connie had to cut down the payroll. Al was under a $100,000 three-year contract, and Mack saw a chance to save the club some money. He sent Al, Mule Haas, and Jimmy Dykes to the Chicago White Sox for $150,000.

Al spent three years in Chicago and made the All-Star team each time. In 1935 he slumped to a poor .267, and that fall his partner of better days, Mickey Cochrane, called him to Detroit. "Black Mike" was now manager of the Tigers. Simmons played one year in Detroit before being traded to Washington.

Al must have thought he was on a merry-go-round for the next few years. It was Boston, Cincinnati, and then—strangely—back to Mack as a spare outfielder and coach. Then he turned up once more with the Red Sox, again came back to the A's as a coach, moved on to Cleveland, and finally retired from the game in 1951.

There was another big honor left. In 1952 his name was added to baseball's Hall of Fame at Cooperstown, N.Y. He was the sixty-fourth player to be enshrined in the diamond pantheon. He deserved the honor.

Mickey Cochrane broke into Mack's line-up on Opening Day at Shibe Park, April 14, 1925. He came up to the plate as a pinch hitter in the ninth inning, cracked out a single to center, and tied the game, which the Athletics later won, 9–8.

That was the major-league debut of probably the greatest catcher the game has ever known. A good receiver and a fine hitter, he was the spark plug of Connie's pennant winners.

"He had more fighting spirit than any man who ever played for me. He was a fighter all the way through," Connie told me. "He was one of the best catchers of all time."

High praise indeed, but Cochrane rated it. For eleven straight years he caught a hundred or more games a season. He had a lifetime batting average of .320. He played in two All-Star games and in 1934 was named Most Valuable Player in his league.

Once he hit three home runs in his first three times at bat, and lost a chance at immortality when Mack pulled him out of the game. It happened on May 21, 1925, at St. Louis. The A's were murdering the St. Louis Browns (they eventually beat them, 20–4); and Mack, thinking to give his regulars a rest, withdrew a number of players, including Cochrane.

Mickey didn't think anything about it at the time. Then he suddenly realized he had had at least two more times at bat coming and just might have hit two more homers.

Cochrane laughed about it later. "That night," he told me, "I met Connie in the lobby of the hotel where we were staying. 'My gosh,' he said, 'I sure pulled one today!'"

Mack sincerely regretted his hasty action. "I've always been sorry about that," he said a quarter of a century later.

But Mickey claims his biggest thrill in baseball came in 1935 when he was catching for and managing the Detroit Tigers. It was the sixth game of the World Series, and the score was tied at 3–3 with the Chicago Cubs at bat in the first half of the ninth inning. Stan Hack led off with a roaring triple, and the Tigers were in trouble. Tommy Bridges, Detroit's ace curve-baller, broke off a pitch that hit the ground two feet in front of the plate. Cochrane made a truly miraculous grab of the ball and held Hack at third.

The courageous Bridges then came in with six snapping curve balls to strike out the next two men. When Augie Galan flied out on a fast ball, the Tigers were out of trouble. Cochrane himself opened the last half of the ninth with a solid one-base hit, went to second on an infield out, and raced for home when Goose Goslin singled to center. He scored the winning run of the World Series.

Gordon Stanley Cochrane was born in Bridgewater, Massachusetts, one of five children of John and Sara Cochrane. He started playing baseball as soon as he was old enough to toddle along a first-base line, and continued right through his school days in Bridgewater.

At Boston University he was known, oddly enough, more for his football prowess than for any notable achievements on the baseball diamond. He was a shrewd quarterback and an excellent kicker; he once booted a long field goal to beat Holy Cross, 3–0.

His professional baseball career started with Dover, of the Eastern Shore League. Mickey considered himself a shortstop or an outfielder, but when he arrived in Dover he found a crisis in full swing. "We need a catcher!" howled the Dover manager.

Mickey had caught only two games in his life, but he was persuaded to go behind the plate. "It's a good thing I could hit," he grinned, "because I sure wasn't much of a catcher. I had lots of trouble, especially with foul balls."

Learning a new position wasn't easy, and it took time. Mainly on the strength of his robust hitting, Cochrane advanced to Portland, of the fast Pacific Coast League. Shortly thereafter he was sold to the Philadelphia Athletics for $50,000.

In the 1925 Philadelphia training camp, Mickey had so much trouble mastering the tricks of catching that Mack toyed with the idea of playing him at third. He was such a fine hitter that he had to be somewhere in the line-up.

But Mickey worked hard—he would catch two hours of batting practice every day—and gradually began to show improvement. He still didn't look like a big-league catcher to most baseball men, but wise old Connie Mack detected something of the spark in the young man. And after that Opening Day pinch hit, Cochrane was the A's' regular catcher. He worked 135 games in his first season.

He still had a lot to learn, however, and a wild throw he made at Boston on April 25 cost the Mackmen a game. Generally speaking, his heavy hitting made up for his other deficiencies.

"He was the life of the party," said Mack with a smile. "Always talking it up. His desire to win led him into arguments sometimes, but mostly they were with opposing players, not umpires."

He was a cocky youngster, and even the great Ty Cobb was not immune to his barbed remarks. One day a Detroit runner was on first when Cobb stepped into the batter's box.

"Take it easy, grandpa, and you won't get hurt," advised the young catcher.

Cobb burned with rage. "Just for that," he snapped, "I'll put on the hit-and-run."

"I'll call for a pitch-out," replied Cochrane.

"Go ahead," said Cobb. "I'll wave to you from first."

Cochrane called for a pitch-out and the ball came in wide of the plate. Just as Cochrane was reaching for the ball and getting set to throw to second to nip the fleeing Tiger base runner, Cobb, the old master, reached across the plate and whacked the ball to right field for a clean single. The runner raced all the way to third, and Cobb stood on first, waving to Cochrane. Mickey didn't taunt the old Tiger much after that.

Mack was in the process of putting together one of his finest teams. But it took time, and the A's were

CONNIE'S KIDS

pennant contenders four years before they finally crashed through in 1929. Cochrane, of course, led the charge. He was smart, too, and knew how to handle pitchers. He spoke softly to Grove and soothed the temperamental southpaw; he lashed out at George Earnshaw and Rube Walberg, made them angry—and he got the best possible pitching out of all three.

A rough young man, Mickey played for keeps. Rival players were quick to realize this and some accepted the challenge. May 15 at Detroit, Harry Heilmann tore down the third-base line in the last of the ninth with the winning run. Cochrane blocked the plate, and the big outfielder crashed into him at top speed. Cochrane dropped the ball and the runner was called safe. But Heilmann had to be carried off the field—he was unconscious.

The Athletics virtually clinched the 1929 pennant on Labor Day when they swept over the World Champion Yankees by 10–3 and 6–5. The first game, as the score indicates, was a walkover, but the second was a thriller. The Yanks, fighting desperately, knocked pitcher Rube Walberg out of the box with a four-run rally in the sixth, and were leading, 5–4, when the A's came to bat in the last of the ninth. Max Bishop socked a double to right and scored the tying run when Mule Haas singled to center. Haas went to second on the throw to the plate. Mickey Cochrane was the next batter, and the Shibe Park crowd went wild when the gritty young catcher crashed a single to right to send Haas home with the winning run. That just about did it. In sparking the A's to a pennant, Cochrane slugged the ball for a .331 average.

The young team was pop-eyed with joy at winning the pennant, and the World Series promised to be the greatest adventure of all. When Mack, getting into the spirit of the occasion, surprised everyone by starting the veteran Howard Ehmke in the first game, even the players were aghast. "Is he going to pitch?" Cochrane asked Mack in bewilderment.

"Yes, Mickey," said the old man, with a smile. "That is, if it's all right with you."

Ehmke, of course, pitched the top game of his career, beating the Chicago Cubs 3–1. After this fast start, the A's were never thwarted. Mickey Cochrane not only hit a cool .400 but also set a Series record for catchers when he was credited with 59 put-outs—thanks, of course, to the strike-out pitching of the Philadelphia hurlers.

Statistically speaking, Cochrane enjoyed his best year in 1930 as the A's raced to another pennant. Mickey hit a terrific .357 and walloped ten home runs. He weighed in with two more circuit blasts as the Mackmen defended their title in the World Series.

He continued his brilliant play through 1931. He was a $20,000-a-year man now, and he earned every cent of it. Still talking it up behind the plate and keeping the whole team on its toes, he sparked the Philadelphians to a third straight pennant. He hit .349 and jumped his home-run production to seventeen.

Mickey had an unhappy time during the 1931

CONNIE'S KIDS

World Series. A Cardinal speedster by the name of Pepper Martin stole everything but Mickey's mask. To make matters worse, Cochrane was ill at the time, but Mack had to use him anyway. In later years, Connie staunchly defended Cochrane's work in that Series. "Everybody blamed poor Mickey," he said, "but it wasn't his fault at all. The pitchers were all letting Martin and others get too much of a lead off first and taking too much time getting the ball off to the plate. There's nothing a catcher can do about that—even a Mickey Cochrane."

Mickey gave Connie Mack two more years of fiery, high-grade catching and heavy hitting. Then, in December, 1933, the Detroit Tigers put in a bid for Cochrane. They wanted him as a playing manager, and they offered Mack $100,000. It was a fine opportunity for Mickey, and Mack needed the money. Reluctantly, he sent his great catcher to the Tigers.

Mickey had a nice set-up in Detroit, and he made the most of it. He was a natural leader, and the men, with few exceptions, followed his orders to the letter.

The Tigers won the 1934 pennant by seven games, and Mickey proudly led his team into the World Series against the St. Louis Cardinals. But he ran into the "Gashouse Gang" at its best and lost out in seven games. It would have taken a superteam to beat the "Gang" in 1934.

Despite their World Series loss, these Tigers were a fine team; and they proved it by seizing the American

League pennant again in 1935. They had a tough fight with the Yankees but outdistanced the New Yorkers after taking two out of three in a crucial series. Then they padded into the World Series against the Chicago Cubs, and, with Cochrane himself banging out six singles and a double, made off with the world championship in six games.

Cochrane ran into nothing but trouble in 1936. First the team bogged down, and then his own health cracked. He had trouble with his eyes and stomach and worked in only 44 games. Even so, the Tigers were able to finish in second place.

There was even more trouble coming up for Black Mike in 1937. On May 25 at the Stadium, his playing career came to an abrupt end. The Tigers at that time were putting up a great fight against the Yankees, and in the third inning Mickey slammed an inside-the-park home run. He almost collapsed after that run—he had given it everything he had. Two innings later Bump Hadley, Yankee right-hander, accidentally hit Cochrane on the head with a fast ball. Mickey instantly fell to the ground. He had a fractured skull, and he spent the next twelve weeks in hospitals. He was only thirty-four years old, but he was through as a player.

The Tigers again finished second to the Yankees; and in mid-August of 1938 Cochrane suddenly severed his connections with the club. According to all reports, his relations with the new Detroit owner, Walter O. Briggs, hadn't been too happy. Briggs had

had one of the best managers in baseball and hadn't seemed to know it.

The baseball world was amazed at the news, but Cochrane himself was probably just as glad to get out from under. He quickly made a business connection with an automobile concern in Detroit, and at one time was said to have a yearly income of around $50,000. Highly intelligent and well educated, Mickey would have been successful at anything. It was baseball's loss.

After the Babe: Lou Gehrig

With the decline and fall of Babe Ruth in the middle 1930's, there passed from the baseball scene the greatest hitter of them all. Not before or since has there been a man who could really fill the shoes of the Babe.

Heir apparent to the throne vacated by the "Sultan of Swat" was his friend and teammate Lou Gehrig. Lou was a mighty hitter and a good first baseman, but he lacked the color, the flair for the spectacular, that made the name of Babe Ruth a byword in homes throughout the nation.

Nevertheless, Gehrig was one of the best who ever played the game. Possibly it's unfair to compare him with Ruth. He followed in the Babe's footsteps as a hero for the New York Yankees, but he left his own mark on the game, his own records in the books.

Gehrig, the durable "Iron Man" who didn't miss a regularly scheduled game in almost fourteen years, was a strapping six-foot 200-pounder. He was powerful enough to present a menacing picture to American League pitchers from the first day he walked onto the field at Yankee Stadium.

He was quiet and serious, and he was not a natural athlete. He had to work hard to perfect a mechanical ability as a first baseman. Gehrig may not have been the best-fielding first sacker the game ever saw, but he was completely adequate. And his high-powered batting would have made up for almost any fielding deficiency. He had a lifetime average of .340, and he was especially deadly with men on the bases. He drove in over 100 runs a season for thirteen years. In 1931 alone, he sent 184 New York runs scooting across the plate. Twenty-three times during his career he came up with the bases loaded and knocked the ball out of the park. One day in Philadelphia he hit four homers in successive times at bat.

Lou played in seven World Series and terrorized National League pitchers, particularly in 1928 when he batted .545 against the St. Louis Cardinals. He hit four homers and knocked in nine runs as the Yanks won in four straight games. Altogether, he drove in 35 runs in World Series competition.

Lou Gehrig was a fine man. Never was there a hint of scandal connected with his name; he seldom even argued with an umpire. He was in every way a credit to baseball. And for his courageous and uncomplaining fight against the terrible disease—multiple sclerosis—that seized him in the latter part of his career and finally claimed his life, Lou won the respect and affection of the whole nation, including people who never went inside a baseball park.

Until he was stricken and dying, he never received the appreciation due him. For some reason players, fans, and writers took for granted his long, booming hits, his steady day-by-day play, and his unassuming good nature. But then, he walked in the shadow of "the King." For during Lou's greatest years, there was always the swaggering, spectacular Babe Ruth to draw the attention of fans and writers. And a couple of years after the Babe came the much heralded wonder boy of the Pacific Coast, Joe DiMaggio. Lou never could get settled in the spotlight. Not that he cared, but he really did deserve it.

Lou worked hard for everything he got—life wasn't easy for the son of Christina and Heinrich Gehrig. He was born June 19, 1903, on the Lower East Side of Manhattan. The Gehrigs were very poor, and Lou's mother had to work in a fraternity house at Columbia University to help support the family. Young Lou became accustomed to helping around the house almost as soon as he was able to walk.

Later he went to public school and took part-time jobs to help solve the family's financial problems. Somehow he also managed to find time for baseball games in the streets, and swimming in the East River.

His introduction to organized baseball came when he entered Commerce High School. The coach put the round, fat youngster with the bashful grin in several different positions, and from all accounts he was equally awkward in all of them. He didn't even appear to be a very strong hitter at that time. But he worked hard, and slowly began to show improvement.

In 1920, the Commerce team won the Public School Athletic League championship of New York and went to Chicago to play Lane Technical School for the P.S.A.L. title.

It was a big thrill for young Lou and the rest of the team to travel by train to Chicago, and they were still nervous and excited when the game started in Wrigley Field. They quickly fell behind but rallied as the game went along. At last Lou came to bat in the ninth inning, with the bases full and the game still hanging in the balance.

The little fat boy swung with all the power he had, which was plenty even then, and knocked the ball out of the park for his first home run. He had won the game—he was a hero. He probably never dreamed then that he would return to the same field twelve years later as a member of the New York Yankees and help crush the Chicago Cubs in a World Series.

Baseball wasn't his only sport in those days. He played football, too, and it was very likely his ability as a line plunger and punter that led to his entering Columbia University. An enthusiastic alumnus watched Lou run another high-school team into the ground and suggested an athletic scholarship.

He had to work hard in preparation for the entrance examinations, but he passed them and entered Columbia in the fall of 1921. His grades were good, considering all the outside activities in which he was involved. He held part-time jobs and played both football and baseball. Although he was a distinguished member of the Light Blue backfield, baseball was rapidly becoming his main area of operations. The coach shifted him around from the outfield to the pitcher's mound to first base, trying to find the best place for him. His fielding was weak, but now he was beginning to hit. One day he smashed out a home run that traveled some 400 feet and broke a window in the Journalism Building. Unknown to Lou, a scout for the New York Yankees, Paul Krichell, was sitting in the stands. He was impressed by the boy's power and thought he saw the makings of a major-league star.

At about the same time, Lou's father became very ill. An operation was needed and there were other heavy medical expenses. The Yankees offered Lou

AFTER THE BABE

$1,500 to sign a contract. It was impossible to say no, even though he would have to leave school.

A few weeks later, Lou reported to Yankee Stadium and met the fabulous stars he had been reading about for years—Babe Ruth, Wally Pipp, Joe Bush, and others of that great aggregation. No wonder Lou was nervous when he took his turn at batting practice. But the great Ruth himself came over and patted him on the shoulder.

"Take it easy, kid!" the Babe boomed.

Lou smiled, regained some of his confidence. A few minutes later he put his powerful shoulders into a swing and lined the ball into the distant right-field stands. After that he was relaxed and "one of the gang."

But he was still just a promising rookie. He needed more seasoning; he also needed a chance to play regularly, which he wouldn't be able to do with the Yankees. Wally Pipp was still too good. Manager Huggins, therefore, sent him off to Hartford.

Lou was unhappy at Hartford. He was in a strange town, away from friends and family. His playing suffered. He fell into a prolonged batting slump, and the Hartford manager wired the Yankees that they might have to take him out of the line-up. The Yankees promptly notified Lou that if he ever expected to get back to New York he'd have to start hitting. Gehrig pulled himself together and began lining hits into outfields all over the Eastern League.

He had one more year in Hartford, and it was a

good one. He hit .369 and collected 37 home runs. There was no denying him now, and when he came back to the Yankees in 1925, he was there to stay.

Wally Pipp had been a great first baseman and a great competitor, but, as all athletes must, he was beginning to fade, and the young and eager Gehrig was waiting on the sidelines. It happened on June 2, in Detroit. That's when Lou took over the spot he was destined to keep for almost fourteen years.

American League pitchers looked the newcomer over carefully, wondering how to pitch to him. They never learned. His bat boomed a serenade of base hits, off the fences and over the fences. With Ruth and Bob Meusel, he formed a triumvirate that became known as "Murderers' Row." Later, with men like Bill Dickey and Joe DiMaggio, he continued to play havoc with the big-league pitchers.

That first year was not a good one for the Yanks—they finished in seventh place; but young Lou hit .295 and rapped out 21 home runs, a little better than good for a first-year man. The following year he got into high gear, and never again hit below .300 until 1938.

In the fall of 1926, Lou played in his first World Series. The Yanks lost in seven games to the Cardinals, but the young first baseman did everything that could be expected of him. He got eight hits, including two doubles, and had a .348 average.

There was no holding the Yanks the next year as Ruth and Gehrig teamed up to furnish the greatest one-two punch in baseball history. Gehrig, hitting at .373, staged a home-run race with the Babe. It was close until September, when Ruth hit 17 in a single month to set his record of 60 for a season. But Lou Gehrig, with 47 out-of-the-park drives, deserves credit for spurring the Babe on.

Although he was now an established star and considerably better off financially, Lou changed but little outwardly. He remained a good-natured, modest, unassuming ball player.

As a boy he hadn't had much time to be interested in girls. He was always too busy working and playing ball. But in 1930, while the Yankees were engaging the White Sox in Chicago, he was introduced to a charming, blue-eyed girl named Eleanor Twichell. Lou was bashful, but after the Yankees had made six or seven more trips to the Windy City, he worked up enough nerve to tell her what was on his mind.

They were married September 29, 1933. The ceremony actually took place a day ahead of schedule. It was planned to be a fairly big wedding, and Lou watched with growing uneasiness the extensive preparations, noted the lists of guests. Finally he could stand it no longer. So they were quietly married with no outside assistance other than that provided by a minister.

On the diamond, Lou, brilliant as he was, still was overshadowed by Babe Ruth. After all, there was only one Babe, the idol of millions. Together they formed a powerful combination, for if one didn't hit, the other would—but more often they both did. They made a shambles of the 1928 World Series, crushing the Cardinals in four straight games. Lou cracked out four home runs, but even then the Babe stole the show with one tremendous burst. In the last game, Ruth lined out three homers in successive times at bat.

Lou's batting fell off somewhat in 1929, when he hit an even .300. In 1930 he was better than ever. He hit .379 and walloped 41 homers while driving in 174 runs. He was "the Crown Prince" to the King—Babe Ruth.

Gehrig was dangerous when men were on the bases. Despite a slightly lower average (.341), he set a league record when he drove 184 runs across the plate in 1931. He went on a home-run binge toward the end of the season. From August 28 to September 1, he hit six home runs in six games, and three of them came with the bases full.

He tied Ruth for homers that year with 46; he would have beaten the Babe except for a somewhat ridiculous incident in a game with Washington. Lyn Lary was on base with two out when Gehrig smashed a drive that just cleared the wall for a homer. Lary took one look at the ball, saw a Washington outfielder in pursuit, and assumed it would be caught. He trotted across the diamond into the dugout. Meanwhile, Gehrig watched the ball disappear, and then, thinking Lary had rounded the bases to score, jogged around to the plate. Washington players claimed Lou was out for passing a base runner; and, of course, the umpire upheld them.

Lou did top the Babe in one respect. Only a handful of men have ever hit four homers in a single game—the Babe never. Yet on June 3, 1932, at Philadelphia, Lou went on a hitting spree that all but wrecked the Athletics. In the first, fourth, and fifth innings he slammed home runs off George Earnshaw, one of the best right-handers in the game. His next time up, he hit another off Leroy Mahaffey. Four home runs in successive times at bat! He nearly made it five in the ninth inning when he unloosed a terrific shot to left field, which Al Simmons grabbed after a long run.

That was Lou's biggest day. Other Yankees had big days, too, and they won the American League pennant easily. Following their old pattern, they trimmed the Cubs in four straight games in the World Series. Lou's contribution: nine hits, including three homers; eight runs batted in and nine scored; and an average of .529.

The following year Gehrig and the fans first began to realize that he was forging a wonderful record of consecutive games played. It is said that a New York newspaperman called Lou's attention to the streak, which at that time had reached more than 1,200 games.

Lou was proud of this record and tried hard to keep it going. There were many days when he should have stayed on the bench—when he was a mass of bruises from crashes on the base paths, when his legs were taped from ankle to knee because of spike wounds. But he never let up, and his booming bat carried the Yankees to more and more victories.

The closest his streak came to being interrupted was on July 14, 1934, in Detroit. The day before, he had been stricken with lumbago and had hardly been able to reach first base on a drive which ordinarily would have been good for at least two bases.

Doctors worked over him that night, but he was in no condition to play the next day. It looked as if the streak was about to be broken. Then manager Joe McCarthy had an idea. Somehow they got him out to the ball park, dressed him, and put him in the starting line-up as lead-off man. He struggled to the plate and, to the amazement of all the Yankees, rapped out a hit. He collapsed when he reached first base, and they carried him back to the hotel. But the streak was intact, and by the next day he was back playing the full nine innings.

The year 1934 was Babe Ruth's last, and Lou now became captain of the team. With the new responsibilities his batting slipped a little, but as always he was a great clutch hitter, driving in 119 runs. In 1936, a new team of stars was forming around him. There were Joe DiMaggio, Bill Dickey, Red Rolfe, Lefty Gomez, Charlie Ruffing, and others. This great aggregation stormed to four straight pennants and world titles, although Lou was only a spectator by 1939.

His last big year was 1937. He hit at a .351 clip,

batted out 37 homers, and sent 159 runners across the plate. It was a real Yankee year, climaxed with a 4–1 victory over the Giants in the World Series. In 1938, for the first time in thirteen years, Lou's average slipped below the .300 mark. He seemed to be losing a little of his old power, but baseball people said that after thirteen years a man was entitled to slow down a bit.

The spring of 1939 was a hard one for Gehrig. Something was wrong. He stumbled occasionally, seemed awkward around first base. At the plate, he couldn't seem to get any power into his swing. Even when he connected solidly the result was usually a feeble fly ball. Manager McCarthy watched him anxiously. So did many other friends. Gehrig himself fought grimly and silently through the spring training session. "I'll get going soon," he seemed to be saying.

The season started with Lou Gehrig on first as usual. But he didn't hit; his fielding fell off. Still, his old friend, McCarthy, wouldn't take him out of the line-up. Finally, on the morning of May 2 in Detroit, Gehrig told his manager that it was time to break the streak. McCarthy nodded. Lou had played 2,130 consecutive games.

He left the team and went to the Mayo Clinic for a checkup. The report, issued June 21, said he was suffering from multiple sclerosis. It was a thunderous blow, but Lou took it with calm courage.

He stayed with the Yankees for a while. He'd take the line-up out to the umpire at home plate, then go back and sit on the bench. Later Mayor LaGuardia had him appointed to the New York State Parole Board. In this capacity he was able to help out a number of youngsters who had got themselves into trouble.

He kept going into his office as long as he could, but death was creeping on. Finally the day came when he could no longer work. He stayed around his house for a month. Then he couldn't get out of bed. He died June 2, 1941, exactly sixteen years after the start of his great streak of consecutive games.

The famous number 4 that he wore on the back of his uniform was retired. No other Yankee will ever again wear that number. In 1942 a movie, *Pride of the Yankees*, based on his life, was released. And up in the Bronx in New York there is now a Lou Gehrig Plaza.

But even without these acts of commemoration, Lou Gehrig could never be forgotten. He was a fine ball player and—what is more important—a fine man.

King Carl: Carl Hubbell

The 50,000 lucky people who sat in on the second annual All-Star game saw something they are probably telling their grandchildren about today. The game, played in 1934 at the Polo Grounds in New York, featured a "spot" pitching exhibition that has never been equaled.

Lined up against a massive array of hitting power for the American League was a defense-minded group of National League ball hawks. Their pitcher was a slender, smooth-working southpaw by the name of Carl Hubbell, and—to the surprise of no one—he was in trouble almost immediately. Charlie Gehringer, of Detroit, smacked a single to right field on the second ball Hubbell threw up. When Heinie Manush drew a base on balls, there were men on first and second with nobody out.

The next three scheduled batters were Babe Ruth, Lou Gehrig, and Jimmy Foxx. It was enough to scare the daylights out of any hurler. It did scare the National League board of strategy, and for a minute they debated the advisability of putting in a new pitcher. Fortunately, they decided against this move, and right then and there Carl Hubbell began to make history. He struck out three of the most feared batters in the game on twelve pitches.

It was an amazing stunt; but Hubbell was just getting warmed up. Two more great sluggers, Al Simmons and Joe Cronin, came up for the Americans in the second inning, and they too went down on strikes. That made it five straight. Bill Dickey broke the spell with a single, but Hubbell quickly fanned Lefty Gomez for the third out.

Hubbell's spectacular feat was the high spot of his great career as a hurler for the New York Giants. He explained it casually enough: "I didn't have to pace myself. I knew three innings was all I was allowed to pitch in an All-Star game anyway, so I just cut loose with everything I had."

One of the greatest southpaws that ever lived, Hubbell won 253 games and lost 154 in his sixteen years with the New Yorkers. He pitched the Giants to pennants in 1933, 1936, and 1937; and in the latter part of his career, when the Giants were a second-division outfit, Carl Hubbell kept right on pitching his heart out every four days. He worked with good Giant teams and he worked with bad ones—but he almost invariably pitched fine ball.

A tall, thin man with a long, narrow face and a somewhat shy smile, Hubbell never lost his composure on the field. He always seemed to have perfect control of himself—and the ball. He once won an eighteen-inning game without giving up a pass, and on another occasion he hurled a no-hitter without giving up a single base on balls. In 1933 he pitched 46 consecutive scoreless innings, and in 1936 and 1937 he put together a winning streak of 24 straight games.

Carl Hubbell served the Giants long and faithfully. And when his arm no longer responded, he was made head of the Giants' farm system. In this job he gave the same serious, studious attention to the game that he had given when he was an active player. And his work paid off in better Giant teams.

Born in Carthage, Missouri, June 22, 1903, Carl Owen Hubbell was a farmer's son. For several years his parents, George and Margaret, had been hearing about the fertile land of Oklahoma, and so when Carl was about three years old they moved their growing family into the new state.

The Hubbell tribe—there were six youngsters—settled near Meeker, and it was at Meeker Public School that Carl had his first experience with baseball. There wasn't much equipment for sports, so the boys played baseball almost all year round. After graduating from high school, Carl took a job with an oil company and pitched for the firm's team in an industrial league. A year later he moved to Cushing of the Oklahoma State (Class D) League. Unfortunately, the league went broke in the middle of the 1924 season, and Carl, who had been losing as many games as he won, joined the Oklahoma City club of the Western League. About a week later he caught typhoid fever and was sidelined for the rest of the season.

During the 1925 season he began to develop the pitch that was to make him famous. He had been having trouble with right-hand hitters, so he took to studying a veteran southpaw who was stopping them with a sinker ball. "This fellow used a side-arm delivery," Carl said, "and I tried to throw the same pitch with an overhand motion. The main idea, of course, was the same—we were both trying to keep the pitch low and make the batters hit on the ground."

Out of this experimentation came the screwball, which, as thrown by a southpaw, is similar to the fadeaway made famous by right-hander Christy Mathewson. Hubbell's pitch came in low and broke sharply away from the batter.

There are no records of Western League operations for 1925, but Carl must have had a good year, for he was sold to the Detroit Tigers at the close of the season.

He was immediately handicapped in his tryout with the Tigers when a Detroit coach ordered him not to throw the screwball. "Too much of a strain," the coach argued. "You'll ruin your arm."

The result was that Carl never had a real chance to show what he could do for the Tigers. They kept him in their farm system for a couple of years, then turned him loose to Beaumont of the Texas League.

Back in the minors once more, Hubbell decided he had nothing to lose and started throwing the screwball again. His arm felt fine, and Texas League batters almost broke their backs trying to hit the elusive pitch.

In June, 1928, Dick Kinsella, a politically conscious scout for the New York Giants, was attending the Democratic National Convention in Houston, Texas. One afternoon, bored with the convention proceedings, he wandered out to the baseball park where last-place Beaumont was playing the league-leading Houston team.

On the mound for the tail-enders was Carl Hubbell, throwing up that screwball. "I was having one of my good days," Carl said. "Everything was working fine and I beat Bill Hallahan, 2–1."

Kinsella forgot all about politics and followed the Beaumont team around for the next week. He saw Hubbell in action twice more and then called John McGraw, manager of the Giants, and told him that he had found a real pitcher. Kinsella's recommendation was good enough for McGraw, and Hubbell was brought up to the Giants at once.

Carl remembered very clearly his first game with the New Yorkers. He joined the Giants in Pittsburgh on July 26 and was thrown in against the Pirates that afternoon.

"I went out there determined not to walk anybody," he recalled with a smile. "I was going to make them hit to the fielders. Well, they hit all right. They hit everything I tossed in and not at the fielders, either. I never got out of the second inning."

The Pirates got him for five runs in that second frame, and Carl returned to his hotel feeling very low. "I had arrived in the city just before the game," he said, "and I hadn't even unpacked my bag. I sure wasn't going to unpack it now! I thought I'd be on my way back to the minors right away. And when McGraw called me into his room the next morning, I was sure of it. But McGraw fooled me, all right. He smiled and said, 'I liked the way you got that ball over the plate. Soon as you learn how to pitch to these National Leaguers, you'll get along fine.'"

After that boost to his morale, Carl Hubbell was a hard man to beat. He did a couple of relief stints, then started against the Phillies and beat them, 4–0.

Hubbell never had anything but kind words for the fiery McGraw, who was as famous for the fights he engaged in as he was for the pennants he won.

"I never had any trouble with him," said Carl. "He was tough but very fair, especially with rookies. The first year he didn't bother you at all, but after that you were supposed to be a big-leaguer and not make mistakes."

McGraw almost had a fit later on during that season. With only a week to go, the Giants, trailing the St. Louis Cardinals by half a game, were playing a double-header with the Chicago Cubs. Hubbell was working for New York, opposed by Art Nehf for the Cubs. It was a tight pitcher's battle, and McGraw's team was behind, 3–2, in the last of the sixth. But when Andy Reese singled and Lester Mann doubled, it looked like a Giant rally.

Frank Hogan, the next batter, hit straight back to Nehf, who whipped the ball to third and caught Reese off the bag. During the run-down, Reese thought he saw a chance to score and dashed for the plate. Gabby Hartnett, the Chicago catcher, had come up the third-base line, and Reese crashed into him. Hartnett threw both arms around the Giant base runner—perhaps to keep from falling. While the pair were struggling, the Cub third baseman walked up and tagged out Reese.

Although McGraw screamed about interference, the decision stood. It cost the Giants that game and very likely the pennant.

Through the following seasons, Carl Hubbell continued to hurl a fine brand of ball for the Giants. On May 8, 1929, he gained fame with a no-hitter against the same Pittsburgh Pirates who had spoiled his debut. And in 1932 he won eighteen games with a team that tied the Cardinals for sixth place. That year, too, he took on the incomparable Dizzy Dean in the first of their exciting hurling duels. Dizzy won this one, 4-2, but in the years to come Carl would more than square the account.

Hubbell was a big name in baseball by this time and a fine drawing card throughout the league. One hot night in St. Louis, he was trying unsuccessfully to get some sleep when the phone rang. A fan was on the other end of the line; he wanted to know if Hubbell was going to pitch that afternoon.

Carl said no, explaining that he had worked the previous day.

"Listen here," said the fan. "Can you give me one good reason why you shouldn't pitch two games in two days?"

"Yes!" shouted Hubbell in exasperation. "I'm not hitting!"

After hammering on the gates for eight years, the Giants finally found the combination in 1933 and seized a pennant. And it was Hubbell, winner of 23 games, who brought them home ahead of the Cardinals.

The turning point in the race came on a Sunday afternoon in the Polo Grounds, when the Giants and Cards squared off for a double-header. Hubbell and Tex Carleton didn't know what they were getting into when they warmed up for that first game. At the end of fifteen tense innings they were right where they had started: incredibly, it was still 0–0. Carleton tired then and Jess Haines came on for the Cards. Finally, in the Giants' half of the eighteenth, Hughey Critz singled and Joe Moore came in from third base with the only run of the game.

Topping off the long day, Roy Parmalee hurled a regulation nine-inning shutout to win the second game for the Giants. The double whitewash meant the pennant for New York.

"I didn't feel particularly tired," Hubbell said later. "During the game a sort of nervous energy keeps you going. After it's all over, that's when you feel tired."

Carl's 1.66 earned-run average was the best in either league, and one of the best ever compiled. And before a jam-packed crowd in the Polo Grounds he got the Giants off winging in the World Series with a 4–2 victory over the Washington Senators. They split the next two games, as Hal Schumacher won for the Giants, 6–1, and Earl Whitehill kept the Senators in the fight with a neat 4–0 win.

Hubbell was back on the hill for New York in the fourth game, and he had to go eleven innings to down the stubborn Washington team, 2–1. Mel Ott hit a home run the next day—and the New Yorkers were World Champs.

The Giants confidently expected to duplicate that year in 1934, but they stumbled in the last month. A chance remark by manager Bill Terry brought on the finishing blow. Said Terry scornfully: "Is Brooklyn still in the league?" This enraged the whole borough of Brooklyn, including the Dodgers. They murdered the Giants at the end of the season and knocked them out of the race. Meanwhile, Dizzy and Paul Dean hurled the Cardinals into the World Series.

After a third-place finish in 1935, the Giants took a leaf out of the Cardinals' book the next year. Trailing the Cubs by nine games in the middle of August, they came on fast to win the pennant. Hubbell, who topped the league with a 26–6 record, won his last sixteen games, including two tense battles with his old rival Dizzy Dean. Each was 2–1, the first going ten innings. Earlier that year he had undergone another marathon with the St. Louis team. Opposed by his old teammate Roy Parmalee, Hubbell went seventeen innings before being defeated, 2–1. And at that, it took an error by the New York third baseman to let in the winning run.

Hubbell had a strange philosophy about these close, stirring games. Yet he made sense when he said, "They aren't the tough ones. Tough games are the ones where you don't have all your stuff, where your control isn't just right and you stagger along from inning to inning, barely getting by. When everything's breaking just right, it's easy. It may be a close game, but it's still easy. Of course, you have to be careful. You make one pitch too good, the batter puts it up in the seats and your ball game is gone."

Although they finished the regular season in fine style, the Giants were overmatched in the World Series. They were pitted against one of Joe McCarthy's great New York Yankee teams, and it's doubtful

KING CARL

if any club could have stood up against that aggregation.

The Series got under way at the Polo Grounds on a cold and windy day. Hubbell and Charlie Ruffing were still warming up when it started to drizzle. As the game progressed, it rained harder and harder.

"Pools of water were all over the place by the third inning," Carl said. "It was hard on the batters and the pitchers. You know how it is—you can't put all your stuff on the ball, and you have to shorten your stride or you'll fall on your face. I never worked a game under worse conditions, and I'm not sure yet how we won it."

But win it they did, 6–1, with a four-run rally in the eighth. After that, however, the Yankees took charge of the Series, winning three straight. They dropped a ten-inning tussle to Hal Schumacher, then wrecked the Giants in the last one, 13–5.

After that fine season of 1936, Carl's salary went up to something better than $20,000 a year. Undoubtedly he earned every penny of it. He earned, too, the nicknames of "King Carl" and "the Meal Ticket."

He started off the 1937 campaign the same way he had finished in 1936, winning his first 8 games, to make it 24 in a row. He modestly told a reporter: "One of these days I'll be out there and I'll be getting my brains knocked out, and I'll wonder how I ever won a game."

That winning streak meant a lot to his teammates, and they did their best to protect it. Once infielder

Lou Chiozza fumbled an easy ground ball and let in a run. He was thoroughly disgusted with himself and almost afraid to go into the dugout at the end of the inning. But Hubbell just grinned at him. Then the Giants went out and won the game anyway.

Carl had another great season, winning 22 and losing 8, and he clinched the pennant for New York with a 2–1 victory over the Phillies. Unluckily, the Giants had to meet the Yankees again in the World Series and were soundly beaten four games to one. The lone Giant win was credited to Hubbell, who whipped the Yanks, 7–3, in the fourth game.

Always even-tempered and fair, the tireless southpaw won the respect of all baseball players and writers. During a wild scene which has been referred to as the "Battle of St. Louis," Dizzy Dean momentarily lost his head and started "dusting off" every Giant who came up to the plate. That is, until he got to Hubbell. Even Dean wouldn't throw at Carl. And once Lefty Gomez, the fine Yankee left-hander, was told that Hubbell was wearing his No. 11 on his uniform. "No," said Gomez. "I'm wearing *his* number."

Hubbell was always glad to help out young pitchers, but he never had much success in teaching them his screwball. "It's pretty hard to teach," he admitted. "In the first place, you just have to be naturally flexible and loose. Otherwise you can't make the pitch behave. The wrist has to be snapped in, and this makes for a good bit of strain."

Of his gameness, his courage under fire, there was never any doubt. No matter what mishaps were occurring on the field, he hurled with the same cool efficiency. For example, there was the day he got off badly against the Dodgers and gave up a home run with the bases full in the first inning. He was four runs behind with the game barely started. But he steadied himself and stopped the Brooklyn attack. A few innings later he hit a home run himself and went on to win the game, 9–5. Once in 1938, he almost pitched another no-hitter despite a sore arm. It was a late-inning single by Tuck Stainback that ruined an otherwise hitless performance against the Phillies.

During the last five years of his career, Hubbell worked with a rapidly disintegrating team. Gradually he began to fade somewhat himself. He didn't seem to have quite the endurance, and his control was no longer perfect—he wasn't "getting the corners." One day against the Cincinnati Reds, he was the Hubbell of old for four innings. In that time he gave up one hit. Then, in the fifth inning, the roof fell in. Two homers, three singles, and an error sent six runs across the plate—and Carl to the showers.

But as late as 1942 he pitched 157 innings to turn in eleven victories against eight losses. And that was when he was thirty-nine years old and had been pitching big-league ball for fifteen years. His last year as an active player was 1943; his last game was a relief chore against the Cubs. And the Giants won the game, 8–7.

That winter he was put in charge of the Giants' farm system. It was no easy job, for the war had depleted many minor-league teams. Hubbell's first task was to set up an efficient scouting staff to uncover promising young players and then to help organize several minor-league teams. He did a workmanlike job, and it wasn't long before potential stars were being drawn into the Giant chain.

Hubbell was ready to settle down. He liked to spend as much time as possible with his wife, Lucille, whom he had married in 1930, and their two sons, Carl Owen, Jr., and James. He also enjoyed an occasional round of golf. But this game was strictly a hobby. With him, nothing could take the place of baseball.

No more cheering throngs, no more autograph hunters—but King Carl didn't care. He had had his fun. Now he was ready to help others make their way to the top.

Not So Dizzy: Dizzy Dean

For eight all-too-short years, fans of the national pastime were delighted by the antics of a big, lighthearted character who, but for an accident at the peak of his career, might have been the greatest pitcher of all time.

Dizzy Dean was a natural. He had everything it takes to be a major-league pitcher: innate ability, unlimited confidence in himself, and a great love of the game. Baseball for him was more than a business, more than a way of making a living. It was the finest of all games; and when he went out there on the mound, he was out to have fun. The fact that a World Series or a pennant might be hanging on his every pitch bothered Ol' Diz not at all.

That's why he was so interesting to watch. You could see him kidding the batter, chatting with a base runner, snapping at an umpire. His big grin was easily discernible from the stands. He was the life of the party, and he wanted everybody, including the spectators, to feel right at home. "Ol' Diz is goin' to be foggin' 'em in there today, and we'll all have fun," he seemed to be saying.

For six years with the St. Louis Cardinals, he was one of baseball's top attractions. He won 133 games in that stretch; and in 1934 he won 30 games, lost only 7, as he and his brother Paul pitched the Cardinals to the world championship. In 1935 and 1936 he won 52 more games—but the following season he was injured in the All-Star game and was never the same again. A line drive caromed off his right foot and broke a toe. Afterward, he tried to pitch favoring the wounded digit, and the resultant strain wrecked his arm.

Baseball was no fun after that, but Dizzy pitched three more years anyway—mostly on courage. He would throw that "nothing ball" up to the plate and dare any batter to hit it. Ultimately, of course, they did just that. When he could no longer come in with that high hard one, Dizzy retreated to the radio booth. His colorful play-by-play accounts from Sportsman's Park in St. Louis, couched in something less than the King's English, made him one of the most popular broadcasters in the country.

When Dean first came up to the majors, he was interviewed in rapid succession by three newspaper reporters. In response to the usual line of questioning, he gave out three different home towns, birthdays, and first names. His only explanation was that he liked all three of the writers and wanted to give each one a scoop! It is reasonably well established now, however, that he was born in Lucas, Arkansas, on January 16, 1911. He was named Jay Hanna Dean, which he subsequently changed to Jerome Herman Dean. The story goes that he took the name of a boyhood friend who died.

He acquired the nickname of Dizzy when, as a minor-leaguer, he beat the Chicago White Sox in an exhibition game. "Why can't you hit that dizzy kid?" snarled the big-league manager to his baffled hired hands. The kid was Dizzy Dean from then on. Actually, of course, he was far from being "dizzy." He was a smart, alert ball player, a shrewd operator who knew he was colorful and knew it would pay off at the box office.

Diz was one of five children of a poor cotton-picking sharecropper whose wife died when Jay Hanna was only three years old. The Dean family moved around the southwest from farm to farm and everybody worked. Diz was doing a man's job when he was only ten years old.

This arrangement didn't leave much time for

formal education, but if Dizzy learned nothing about algebra and Latin, he did pick up something about the geography of the United States by the simple expedient of traveling around the country. And he learned how to get along with all kinds of people, which, when you come down to it, is important, too.

Diz's father, Albert, had been a semi-pro baseball player in his younger days, and whenever there was a spare moment he had the boys throwing a ball around. Diz didn't really start pitching, however, until he joined the Army. Only sixteen at the time, he hurled for the 12th Field Artillery team at Fort Sam Houston in Texas.

But the discipline even of a peacetime army didn't sit too well with the big youngster, so he left after three years and signed up with a semi-pro team in San Antonio. The very next year he won sixteen straight games, and an alert St. Louis Cardinal scout picked him up.

Sent to St. Joseph in the Western League, Diz was an immediate hit. He won seventeen, lost only eight, and was promoted to Houston in the Texas League. His first start at Houston was a 12–1 victory, and it is said that he afterward apologized to the Houston owner for allowing that one run.

Near the close of the 1930 season the Cardinals brought him up for a quick look at some major-league batters. It was September 28 when Dizzy Dean made his first start in the big leagues. He was twenty years old at the time, a tall, lean fellow with wondrous speed and good control.

You might think the boy would be nervous. Not Diz. From the very beginning he had all the poise and assurance in the world. Facing a hard-hitting Pittsburgh Pirate club, he gave up two hits in the first inning, then settled down and allowed but one more hit throughout the remainder of the game. He struck out five, walked three—and won his game, 3–1.

He was a cocky youngster anyway, and there was no holding him after that victory. He breezed into the Cardinal training camp the next spring and announced that he would pitch the Cards to a pennant if they would let him work often enough. He might have, at that, but Gabby Street was managing the St. Louis club and the antics of this fresh kid pleased him not at all. During an exhibition game with the World Champion Philadelphia Athletics, Street thought he saw a chance to put the boy in his place. The powerful A's were putting on a rally when Street told Dean to go in and stop them. Gabby settled back with a grin. But he was sadly disappointed. The confident youngster quickly fanned Al Simmons and Jimmy Foxx, two mighty hitters, and went on to win the game.

In spite of this great work, Dean didn't stay with the Cardinals in 1931. The club was loaded with talent that year, and Gabby Street decided he could get along without Diz for another season. As it turned out, he was right, for the Cards went on to win the pennant. As for Diz, he went back to Houston, where he won 26 games and lost only 10.

Actually, that extra year in the minors was the best thing in the world for Dean. In Houston he met Patricia Nash and married her a week later. Through the years she always exerted a steadying influence on the irrepressible Diz.

By 1932, Diz could no longer be denied a big-league berth. St. Louis brought him up and kept him. Although the Cards slipped from their high post of Champions and wound up in a sixth-place tie with the New York Giants, it was a fine first year for Dean. His 286 innings were the most pitched by any hurler in the league. He led in strike-outs with 191. He won 18 games, 3 of them against the Giants in the space of five days. In his sophomore year in the majors he won 20 games, yanked the Cardinals up to fifth place, and set a National League strike-out record.

The year 1934 was Dean's greatest—probably as good a year as anybody ever had. His brother Paul had been brought up by the Cards, and between them the two Deans overpowered the league. Dizzy's pride in his younger brother was almost pathetic. Paul was the opposite of Diz. A quiet, modest, hard-working young fellow, he was a good ball player, but he wasn't up to Dizzy when it came to mowing down the opposition. Nevertheless Diz used to say, "Paul is even faster'n me." And he promised everybody that

"Me an' Paul" would win 45 games that season. Diz was wrong on that point. They won 49, and they pitched the Cardinals to the pennant in one of the most thrilling races the National League has ever seen.

This St. Louis club was the "Gashouse Gang," a famous and colorful aggregation the baseball world will never forget. Managed by Frankie Frisch and inspired by the antics of Pepper Martin, Dizzy Dean, Leo Durocher, and half a dozen others, the Gang was a hard-running, hard-fighting team. On the field they fought like tigers for every game, and off the field they sought just as earnestly for excitement and laughter.

Frankie Frisch must have acquired many a gray hair handling that outfit. Once during a dull evening at Philadelphia, Dean, Martin, and a couple of accomplices invaded a private dining room of the hotel at which they were encamped. Disguised as workmen and armed with ladders and hammers, they began noisily to remodel the room. The dignified guests were shocked at first. Then they discovered it was just a gag and invited the players to have dinner with them.

Another time Frisch was standing outside a hotel when a paper bag filled with water hurtled to the street, missing him by inches. Frank bolted back into the hotel, sure that it was either Martin or Diz. He cornered Martin and wrung a confession from him. The story goes that Martin promised to atone for his misdeed by hitting a homer the next day. He did it, too. That was life with the Gashouse Gang.

Some of their antics weren't so funny. Once during the 1934 season, Dizzy balked at pitching an exhibition game, and he and Paul went on a strike. There was something to be said for their action. They were, of course, great attractions, and the Cardinal management, never an organization to overlook a few extra dollars, booked numerous exhibition games despite the fact that the Cards were involved in a tough pennant fight. Naturally, "Me an' Paul" were expected to appear at these games and pitch a few innings. The Deans rebelled and went home. But their love of the game was too much. They turned up a week later and went back to work as though nothing had happened.

After a slow start in 1934, the Gang got rolling in August and scrambled into the battle for first place. But when they dropped a Labor Day double-header to the Pittsburgh Pirates, it looked as though their main chance was gone.

On September 13, they moved into Brooklyn for an important double-header with the Dodgers. In a clubhouse meeting before the first game, Frisch was running down the Dodger batting order, giving detailed instructions on how to handle each man. Dizzy, who was scheduled to work the opener, leaned against the wall. Lazily he straightened up and interrupted his boss.

"Shucks, Frank," he drawled, "you know this is a

NOT SO DIZZY 107

waste of time. Why, these guys could never beat Ol' Diz."

Frisch threw up his hands in disgust and sent his Cardinals out on the field. It is safe to say that if he hadn't been battling for a flag, Frank would just as soon have seen the Dodgers hammer Dean out of the park.

But look what happened! Going into the eighth inning, Diz had a no-hitter, but he was so busy having fun and laughing at Frisch that he didn't know it. And, of course, the old baseball superstition wouldn't let any of his teammates tell him. The theory is that if the no-hitter is mentioned, it will vanish when the next enemy slugger steps up to the plate. Even a radio reporter doing a play-by-play account of the game would hesitate to mention the fact for fear of putting the "whammy" on it.

In the eighth, the Dodgers got to Diz for a couple of inconsequential singles, and another in the ninth. This meant nothing to Dean since the Cards were way out in front; they won the game by 13–0. Diz didn't know till it was all over how close he had come to the Hall of Fame.

He didn't care until a few hours later. Brother Paul went out to pitch the second game and, paying strict attention to business, he came through with a blazing no-hitter to win, 3–0. Diz was irked then. "I wisht Paul hadda tol' me he was gonna pitch a no-hitter," he said. "I'da thrown one myself in the first game. That woulda been some record!"

In the final week of the season it was Dean, Dean, Dean, and Dean again, as the incomparable duo swept St. Louis to the pennant. On September 25, Diz beat the Pirates, 3–2. Then Paul dropped a close one, and Diz came back with two days' rest to blank the Cincinnati Reds, 4–0, and tie the New York Giants for first place. On September 29, Paul won, 6–1; and the next day, the last of the season, Diz beat the Reds, 9–0. It was his thirtieth win of the year and his seventh shutout. Paul had won 19 games—so between them the Dean boys had accounted for 49 victories.

They weren't ready to go home yet. There was the little matter of a World Series with Mickey Cochrane's Detroit Tigers. The series opened in Detroit on a Tuesday, and naturally it was Dizzy Dean on the mound for the Cardinals. He had just pitched on Sunday; he had been throwing his arm off for the past two months; and now for the first time in his life he was in a World Series. All that meant absolutely nothing to the confident, rubber-armed Dizzy. It was strictly no-contest as Diz sneered at the American League sluggers, sent his fast ball whizzing over the corners of the plate, and beat the Tigers, 8–3.

Frisch tried to get by in the second game without using a Dean, and this error in judgment allowed the Tigers to tie up the series. The younger Dean went in to pitch the third game, and he put the Cards back into the lead with a 4–1 win.

Both Deans were on the bench again as the fourth game started, and a quartet of other St. Louis hurlers took a neat pasting from the Tigers, who won, 10–4. Diz broke into the game in spectacular fashion when he was called on by Frisch as a pinch runner. Frank was criticized in many quarters for taking such a chance with his star pitcher, but Diz was such a great competitor that Frisch probably thought his mere presence in the game might get the Gang started.

The Cardinals might very easily have lost the Series right then and there. Diz went into second like a runaway locomotive, and a Detroit infielder, trying for a double play, hit him on the head with the ball. Knocked unconscious, Diz was carried from the field while more gray hairs sprouted on the Frisch cranium. Fortunately, Diz quickly recovered his senses, inquired if the double play had been broken up, and went about his business.

Whether or not he was still bothered by that whack on the head, Dizzy did lose a ball game the next day. Tommy Bridges, Detroit's fine curve-baller, beat him, 3–1, and the Tigers needed only one more game for the championship. With the next two contests scheduled for Detroit, the Cardinals were in a difficult spot. But the Gang was used to tough spots.

When Paul Dean shaded Schoolboy Rowe for his second Series win, the classic was tied at three apiece. There was never any serious doubt about the identity of the St. Louis pitcher for the seventh and deciding game. It was a natural for Dizzy. He strutted to the mound before a wild Detroit crowd and made kittens out of the Tigers.

By the ninth inning the Cardinals were ahead 11–0. Dizzy was enjoying himself tremendously. He laughed at the Detroit fans and insulted the sullen Tigers. In the ninth, with one on and one out, Hank Greenberg, Detroit's great slugger, stepped up to the plate. Diz kept fiddling around, baiting Greenberg and delaying the action. At last, Frisch, who was never completely happy until there were three out in the ninth, told Diz to go back to work or he would take him out of the game. At the same time, he dispatched four pitchers to the bull pen to warm up in a hurry. This, with the score 11–0 and baseball's top pitcher on the mound.

Somewhat surprised, Diz settled down to business. He finished striking out Greenberg and ended the game a few minutes later.

The World Series was over, the Cardinals were Champs, and their star pitcher was tired out. For his truly spectacular work that year, Dizzy Dean deserved the Most Valuable Player award, and he got it. He was also honored by the nation's baseball writers, who voted him Player of the Year. Undoubtedly he was.

The year 1935 was another great one for "Me an' Paul" as they racked up a total of 47 victories for the Cardinals. It was almost—but not quite—enough for another pennant. Diz won 28 and Paul 19, but the Chicago Cubs came on with a record-breaking streak of 21 straight wins and nosed them out of the race. It was a tough one for the Gashouse Gang to lose,

NOT SO DIZZY 111

particularly since they had led the league most of the way.

Diz continued his brilliant work through the next year; but Paul's arm went lame, and he was never again as effective as he had been for those two years. Diz himself won 24 and lost 13 as the Cards tied the Cubs for second place.

The turbulent career of Jerome Herman Dean hit a high spot in 1937 when he went to the mat with Ford Frick, president of the National League. It all started in St. Louis one May afternoon when Diz found himself involved in a tight duel with Carl Hubbell and the New York Giants. Covering first in an early-inning play, Diz crashed into a Giant base runner. Both went down and got up swinging. In a matter of seconds, players of both clubs were slugging it out in what was later termed the "Battle of St. Louis." As usual when ball players start swinging their fists, nobody was badly hurt.

The umpires finally got the contestants separated and started the game again. Things were relatively quiet for a few innings, and then an umpire called a balk on Dizzy which led to the winning run. Diz hit the roof—but the Giants had won the game. A few nights later, Dean attended a banquet and, in the course of making a speech, threw in a few derogatory remarks about Frick and his National League umpires.

The remarks were recorded by the press and soon reached the sensitive ears of the National League prexy. Dizzy was suspended, and as soon as the Cards reached New York on their next eastern trip, he was called onto the carpet at the league headquarters. He was handed a severe reprimand and asked to sign an apology to Frick and the umpires.

Highly indignant, Diz stormed out of the office with his now famous remark, "I won't sign nuthin'!" He never did, either. His suspension was up on the last day of the New York series, and Frisch sent him to the mound against the Giants. Again opposed by Carl Hubbell, and with the boos of the Giant fans ringing in his ears, Diz was unbeatable. He allowed only three hits as he easily trimmed the New Yorkers, 8–1. That was Dizzy Dean—when things were toughest he was at his best.

Whenever baseball fans or writers get together and start trading stories, there are sure to be at least a couple of Dizzy Dean anecdotes thrown around. Some of them may be hearsay, but Diz was the kind of character to whom such things *could* have happened.

There was the time, for example, when he was warming up for a game in Boston and announced to the enemy bench that he was not going to throw a curve all day. He promised them nothing but fast balls. Now, telling a big-leaguer that all he had to worry about was straight balls would be suicide for an ordinary pitcher. But Dizzy was no ordinary pitcher. He not only kept his promise but threw a shutout in the process.

Another time he bet a friend he would strike out Vince DiMaggio, of the Boston Braves, the first time he came up. He did it, all right, and his friend offered to double the bet that he couldn't do it again. Again DiMaggio went down on strikes. They kept it up till Diz had fanned poor Vince four straight times. Once the luckless DiMaggio lifted a short foul back of the plate and Diz, in anguished tones, howled to his catcher to let it go. Fortunately the ball hit on the screen anyway.

Diz visited a children's hospital one day and during a conversation asked one of the youngsters what he could do for him. "Strike out Bill Terry with the bases full," the boy commanded. This was a large order—Terry was one of the most consistent hitters in the league. But Diz never hesitated. "All right," he said.

That afternoon at the end of eight innings he hadn't been able to get Terry up there with three on. So, in the ninth, he purposely passed three men to get at Terry and struck him out on three straight pitches. Well, that's the story—and it *could* have happened.

Ol' Diz worked in four All-Star games, and it was the last one that brought the sad ending to his great pitching career. In Washington on July 7, 1937, he was on the hill for the Nationals and having his usual good time at the expense of the American League. Then Earl Averill, of the Cleveland Indians, caught hold of a fast ball and rammed it back through the box. It hit Diz on the left foot and broke a toe. That did it.

He tried to come back and take his turn for the Cardinals before the bone had mended. In order to spare the toe, he took to using a different motion which threw the strain on a different set of muscles. It ruined his arm and he was never again the same pitcher.

He was only twenty-six years old at the time, and it was thought that with rest he might easily come back. But some people guessed the truth. Among them was not Phil Wrigley, owner of the Chicago Cubs. Although Dean won only thirteen games in 1937, Wrigley bought him from the Cardinals for $185,000 and three other players. It was one of baseball's biggest deals.

Wrigley didn't get the pitcher he thought he was getting, but he claimed later that he didn't lose on the bargain. Diz was still a fine attraction, and his fighting spirit had a lot to do with the Cubs' victory in 1938. As for Diz, he grinned and said he was happy to go with the Cubs. Actually, it did mean more money for him. But the Gashouse Gang was never the same afterward.

Probably Dizzy knew he would never again be a big winner, but he wouldn't quit. His speed and curve were gone, but he had a lot of nerve left. "Ol' Diz can still stop these guys," he would say grimly. And sometimes he did.

For most of the 1938 season, it looked as though the Pittsburgh Pirates would take the National League crown. In fact, they went so far as to build additional seats in anticipation of a World Series in the Smoky City. But the Cubs, led by a fine catcher, Gabby Hartnett, kept driving right down to the finish line. The pennant was decided in a crucial series at Chicago late in September. Dizzy Dean started the first game and teased the Pirates for eight innings. He was leading, 2–0, and had two men out in the ninth inning before he had to be relieved.

Next day Hartnett all but won the flag with a game-clinching ninth-inning homer, and then the Cubs went on to make it three straight with a smashing 10–1 triumph.

Ol' Diz, bad arm and all, was back in the World Series again. He sat on the bench in the first game and watched the New York Yankees turn back the Cubs, 3–1. Then he went out there himself in the second game to see what could be done about evening up the Series. A fluke single with two on meant two runs for the Yankees in the second, but Joe Marty's clutch hitting gave the Cubs one in the first and two in the third. Diz held grimly to his 3–2 lead. Inning after inning, he cagily turned back the slugging New Yorkers. At the end of seven innings, he still held his margin; he had allowed but three hits. It was a tense game, and fans everywhere were rooting for Ol' Diz to come through.

He came so close that it was heart-breaking to watch what followed. In the eighth inning the ax fell. Frank Crosetti, not one of the harder-hitting Yankees, pulled a drive into the left-field stands with one on. Dizzy's heart sank as he watched that long fly going deeper and deeper, finally dropping into the seats. In the next inning Joe DiMaggio's homer, also with one on, was anticlimactic. The Cubs lost, 6–3.

Diz made a brief appearance in the last game of the Series. The Yanks were attacking bitterly in the eighth inning, and Dean had to come in and put out the fire. But it was too late, and the Yankees swept the Series.

Dizzy stayed around for a couple more years. He won six games in 1939 and three in 1940. In between, he tried a stretch in the Texas League, hoping that the heat and regular work would bring back the strength and cunning to his arm. It didn't work out that way. Now he was through.

Unable to play ball anymore, Dizzy did the next best thing. He climbed into a broadcasting booth and went on the air to tell the St. Louis fans, in his own amazing style, what was happening to the Browns and Cardinals on the field.

It was tragic that his pitching career was cut so short, for there was never a better pitcher than the Dizzy Dean of those six years with the Cardinals. Ol' Diz had just about everything.

Indian Chief: Bob Feller

Before the start of the 1948 season, most baseball experts agreed that the American League race would be a two-team affair. They didn't feel that any team could possibly threaten the Boston Red Sox and the New York Yankees.

Their predictions didn't stand up too well, though; for most of the season it was a four-team race as Cleveland and Philadelphia joined the Yanks and Red Sox in an exciting fight for the flag.

When the smoke had cleared, it was found that the Cleveland Indians had nailed down the pennant, but only after ambushing the Red Sox in the first play-off game in American League history. The Indians then whacked the other Boston entry, the National League Braves, in the World Series, and were Champions of the baseball universe.

The most significant aspect of Cleveland's first title in twenty-eight years was that it gave baseball's most widely heralded pitcher the chance to hurl in a World Series.

For a dozen years Bob Feller had been winning great numbers of games for Indian teams that were second-rate or worse. Victor in more games than any hurler of his generation, Bob had pitched two no-hitters and ten one-hitters. He even broke the league strike-out record when he fanned 348 batters in 1946. To put it briefly, he was generally considered the best pitcher in either league.

His case was similar to that of Walter Johnson, who toiled so faithfully for the Washington Senators in one lost cause after another. Now Bob had his chance; and, like the great Walter, he had a bitter experience in the fall classic.

Feller was charged with the only two losses the Indians suffered in the Series, but with a little luck he might well have won the first game and sent the Indians on their way to a four-game sweep. Surely on that first day he pitched well enough to win nine out of any ten games.

The Series got under way at Boston, and Bob dueled through seven thrilling innings with Johnny

INDIAN CHIEF

Sain of the Braves. It was 0–0 in the last of the eighth when Bob gave up a base on balls to Bill Salkeld, Boston catcher. Phil Masi was put in to run for Salkeld, and moved to second when Feller was unlucky enough to walk the weak-hitting Eddie Stanky.

Then came the most disputed play of the whole year. The Indian infield had developed a very slick pick-off play that had worked well during the regular season. Manager and shortstop Lou Boudreau flashed the sign to his catcher, who relayed it to the mound. Bob Feller counted slowly to himself: "1-2-3-4." Then he whirled and blazed the ball to Boudreau, who put it on Masi.

It was a close play—there has never been a closer one—and the umpire called the Boston runner safe. A violent argument ensued, but the umpire refused to change his decision. When play was resumed, Tommy Holmes got the second hit off Feller. It was a clean single and scored Masi with the only run of the game.

The controversial play caused no end of talk among fans and sports writers. Even the pictures failed to present a satisfactory answer. Boudreau and his Indians complained bitterly, then went back to work and won the Series. Feller, chief victim of the decision, had practically nothing to say. He took it with a quiet smile—yet it must have been a brutal disappointment, for it deprived him of a World Series victory. And he had pitched a really brilliant game.

When he came back in the fifth game he was not himself at all. The Braves hit him hard and often, and knocked him out of the box in the seventh inning.

It was Bob's misfortune that when he finally got his big chance he was unable to produce a winning effort. Yet without him, Cleveland never would have climbed into the Series. When the Indians began to slip in August, Robert stepped in. He won seven of nine starts, and saved two other games with heady relief pitching. The Indians, regaining their balance, went on to win.

The Bob Feller story has been told in great detail many times. For our purposes it is enough to say that he was an outstanding and well-paid athlete. For many years he labored for a Cleveland club that was seldom even a pennant contender. During that time he was often plagued by nonsupport at the bat and in the field. Yet despite the fact that Cleveland hitters weren't hitting and Cleveland fielders weren't fielding, Bob went right on pitching his heart out. He won numerous games, recorded numerous strike-outs—and, incidentally, made the Cleveland owners pay and pay.

He made more money out of baseball than any other man of his time. Every year Cleveland officials held their heads when they signed the smiling fireballer to a contract. His 1948 contract, for example, called for a base pay of $40,000 plus a bonus on attendance at home games. Since the pennant-winning Indians broke all attendance records, Feller's

INDIAN CHIEF

pay must have been better than $90,000. In this respect he topped even Babe Ruth, although it must be admitted that Bob had to pay out more in taxes.

Feller was very canny about money matters. He was a great drawing card, he well knew, and he made the Indians reimburse him accordingly. But that wasn't all. Extracurricular activities included such items as post-season exhibition games and several ghostwritten books. He lent his name—for a price— to sporting-goods concerns, food companies, and hair-tonic manufacturers. He was a farm boy who never went to college, but he knew a lot about finance.

In a sense, he earned every dollar he ever made, for he was very good indeed. To watch him at his best was to see a craftsman in action. Bob seemed to take charge of a ball game. He had confidence and poise, and seemed to know what was going to happen on every pitch. He might get behind on a batter—run up a count of two or three balls—but even then you didn't have the slightest feeling that the batter was likely to get on base. Bob would come in with his blazing fast ball or the bewitching curve he developed in later years, and the count would soon be even. Then the chances were better than good that the batter would either strike out or pop up.

Take the game on April 30, 1946. Feller faced Floyd Bevens in a tight duel at Yankee Stadium. The erratic Bevens was having one of his good days, and for eight innings he held the Indians scoreless. Feller had a tougher task—he was up against the slugging Yankees. But over the same span the New Yorkers were also runless—and hitless!

Came the ninth inning, and Frank Hayes, Feller's battery mate, rammed a high drive into the left-field stands for a home run. It was the first run of the game. In the last half of the ninth, George Stirnweiss was safe on an error by the Indian first baseman, and the New York fans began to yell. Tommy Henrich, Joe DiMaggio, and Charley Keller were the next three hitters. Now was the time to crack through Feller. Henrich bunted, and the fleet Stirnweiss moved to second on the sacrifice. Up stepped Joe DiMaggio, hero of many a last-ditch Yankee rally. Great hitter that he was, DiMaggio couldn't solve Feller in this clutch. His best effort was a sharp ground ball to Boudreau.

Now Feller was one out away from victory. He worked slowly and carefully on Keller, a very rough left-handed hitter. A minute later even the Yankee fans were cheering Bob, because Keller grounded meekly to the Indian second baseman and the game was over. Feller had another no-hitter. That was Bob Feller at his best—a cool and tremendously effective workman.

Robert was born in Van Meter, Iowa, November 3, 1918. Van Meter is a small town, and Bob spent most of his early youth on a nearby farm where he developed the powerful muscles that were to serve him so well in the years to come.

He started playing baseball in school and soon showed a blazing fast ball that could hardly be seen, let alone hit. Semi-pro teams in the vicinity had the same difficulty with this teen-aged farm boy as his school opponents had had. One day a Cleveland scout showed up and, after a deal somewhat complicated by Bob's youth and the fact that he had no minor-league experience, got him into a Cleveland uniform.

He was seventeen years old when he made his first start in the major leagues. He won it, too, and fanned fifteen of the St. Louis Browns in the process. A couple of weeks later this amazing youngster faced the Philadelphia Athletics and tied a strike-out record set by Dizzy Dean in 1933: he struck out seventeen of the bewildered Philadelphians.

Baseball players and followers were amazed. It didn't seem possible that a mere boy could throw a ball with such tremendous speed and power. He was a sensation, and fans began to pack parks all over the league to see the "boy wonder" in action. His only problem at this time appeared to be control—or rather, lack of it. And in a way even this worked to his advantage, for batters, leery of his speed, had to be ready to duck or drop to the ground. In other words, they couldn't "dig in" at the plate and swing away.

Despite his great strike-out routine, Bob didn't, of course, win all his games. There were times when his wildness got him in trouble, and other times when a batter, swinging blindly, rapped out a base hit. In 1936 and 1937 Bob won fourteen games while losing ten. Actually, it wasn't until 1938 that he really got into his stride. That year he won seventeen and lost eleven, and pulled the Indians into third place. During this, his third year with the Tribe, he broke his own strike-out record when he fanned eighteen of the hard-hitting Detroit Tigers.

From 1939 through 1941 he was the outstanding pitcher in baseball. Gaining control over that hopping fast ball, he won 76 games and lost 33 in the three-year stretch. He opened the 1940 season with a no-hit conquest of the Chicago White Sox. It was his first no-hitter, and the first ever pitched on Opening Day.

Then came Pearl Harbor, and for almost four years Bob served in the United States Navy. He was discharged from the Navy in time to pitch a few games for the Indians in 1945, and appeared to have lost little of his effectiveness.

The following year he looked better than ever. Working a grand total of 371 innings, he won 26 games and lost 15 for a sixth-place club. He fanned 348 batters to break Rube Waddell's old record, and, in addition to his classic no-hitter against the Yankees, he also turned in a pair of brilliant one-hit jobs. On July 31, Bobby Doerr's single was the only hit the Red Sox could get as Feller beat them 4–1. Little more than a week later, August 8, the White Sox gathered one safe blow and were beaten 5–0.

INDIAN CHIEF

People said he was slipping in 1947 when, with a mediocre club in back of him, he won only 20 games. That, however, is a season figure most pitchers never achieve, so the complaints of the fans actually amounted to a tribute to Feller.

Bob took time to set up two more one-hitters in 1947. On April 22, against the St. Louis Browns, he turned in one of the finest exhibitions ever seen. For six innings the Brownies couldn't even put a man on first base. Then with one out in the seventh, Al Zarilla, St. Louis outfielder, reached across the plate for a curve and popped it into center field for a single. That broke the tension, but Bob kept right on blazing them in. He walked a man in the ninth, but that was the extent of the St. Louis offensive operations. Bob fanned ten and won the game by a 5-0 score.

A short time later he faced the Red Sox, a far more dangerous team than the Browns. The second man up in the first inning, Johnny Pesky, belted him for a base hit. Then Bob shut the door, and the Sox were turned back without another hit for the rest of the afternoon. This was the third time he had held a Boston team to one hit.

In the final drive for the 1948 pennant, Feller again picked on the heavy-hitting Red Sox. On September 22, some 77,000 fans came out to see the Indians meet the Bostonians in Cleveland. The Indians had to win, for Boston was leading by a game. Bob Feller got the call, and, with a pennant hanging on every pitch, he set the Sox down in order for five innings, allowed only three hits, and won his game, 5–2. Big gun in the Indian attack was Ken Keltner, who homered in the first inning with two men on base.

Four days later Feller faced Hal Newhouser at Detroit—and remember, every game was vital to the Indians, no matter whom they were playing. Feller allowed only five hits and did not walk a single batter as he pitched the Indians into a one-game lead with a 4–1 victory.

Bob Feller kept on winning games for the Indians. In 1951 he won 22, and one of them was a no-hitter (his third) against the Detroit Tigers. He was always a cool and courageous performer, and it is no wonder he is considered one of the most effective pitchers the game has ever known. He retired after the 1956 season, but the fast-throwing Iowa farm boy with the mind of a financial wizard will be remembered as one of the very best in this great business.

Yankee Clipper: Joe DiMaggio

One of the greatest center fielders in baseball history began his sparkling career on a sunny spring day in 1936 in New York's Yankee Stadium. It was Opening Day, and fans got their first look at a slim, black-haired twenty-two-year-old rookie who was destined for a hero's role in many a Yankee triumph during the next fifteen years. This was the swift-running, hard-hitting Joe DiMaggio. Mel Allen, the radio announcer who broadcast play-by-play reports of Yankee games for two decades, called him "the Yankee Clipper."

From his very first game in the big leagues, the handsome DiMaggio owned center field at the Stadium—there was never any question about it. He appeared to float over the greensward, never seemed to be running hard. Yet he was always in the right place when the ball came down. He made the most difficult chances look almost easy. And he did it day after day, year after year.

At the plate, he was, of course, something better than good. Twice he was the American League batting champion and twice the home-run champion. In 1941, he shattered a forty-five-year-old record when he hit safely in 56 straight games. Three times he was awarded the Most Valuable Player plaque.

A cool, efficient operator, DiMaggio appeared to be somewhat aloof from fans and players alike. Baseball was a job, although it came easily to him and he never had to put in long, hard hours learning the game the way Lou Gehrig did. Although he was machine-like in his perfection, he was not without emotion; he was capable of anger, despair, and elation.

Joe was born November 25, 1914, in Martinez, California, of Italian-born parents. He started playing ball on the sandlots, and quit high school at the age of seventeen to join the San Francisco Seals of the Pacific Coast League. This was fast company, but Joe was a natural ball player. He didn't have to stop and think what to do on the diamond—he did the right thing instinctively.

YANKEE CLIPPER

When he joined the Yankees in 1936, he was the most highly publicized rookie of the year. But he made his press notices stand up from the beginning.

He started out fast, perhaps too fast. He hit two homers in one inning in June, had a fourteen-game hitting streak, and was a solid attraction everywhere he went. On top of that, the Yankees were leading the league.

Then it happened. Although he was a first-year man, his playing had been so excellent that he was chosen for the All-Star game. The confident rookie had a terrible day. In the field he misplayed a line drive, fumbled a ground ball, and altogether was implicated in the scoring of three National League runs. At the plate he failed miserably—he never got the ball out of the infield in five attempts. And his team lost, 4–3. It was the worst game of baseball he ever played.

He played so many good ones, however, that it would take several volumes to record them all. In 1937, he once hit for the cycle: a homer, triple, double, and single. Another day in his second year, he hit three homers in one game. His season average was .346, and he led the league in home runs with 46.

In the first game of a double-header with Cleveland the following season, 1938, he broke a record when he hit three triples in successive times at bat. The first one came in the sixth inning when the Yanks were stumbling along with a 3–0 deficit. Joe came up with two out and Red Rolfe on first. He smashed a high, hard drive that cleared Earl Averill's head in center field.

Possibly inspired by this show of power on the part of their batting ace, the Yankees drove back for three more runs in the next inning and took a 4–3 lead. DiMaggio led off in the eighth, again slammed a mighty three-base hit, and subsequently scored on a fly to the outfield.

Now it was 5–3, and the spectators were beginning to think of the hot dogs they would try to get between games. But the Indians had other matters in mind. They stormed back with four runs—the result of two singles, a Yankee infield error, a triple (this game was full of them), and a fly ball.

The New Yorkers were chagrined. Instead of having the ball game in their collective pocket, they found themselves in the awkward position of trailing by two runs with only three outs left to them. However, they still had DiMaggio.

There were two out and a man on first when the storm broke and sent the Indians scurrying into the wigwam. Rolfe and Tommy Henrich put together a pair of singles to score one run and bring up DiMaggio.

Onlookers were surprised to note that Averill did not move back to the base of the flagpole in center field. You would think he'd have learned by this time. For sure enough, DiMaggio again laced into the ball and sent it screaming over Averill's head for another

YANKEE CLIPPER

three-bagger that scored two runs and won the ball game, 8–7.

The second half of the twin bill was exciting, too, but this time most attention was focused on the pitcher's box. Monte Pearson, Yank right-hander, pitched that much-to-be-desired item, a no-hitter. The game itself was never in doubt. The New Yorkers went out in front with a five-run rally in the first inning and won, 13–0. It was a great day for Joe and Monte.

DiMaggio had become a top-ranking star of a championship team, so his salary began to jump accordingly. He received an estimated $27,500 for his toil in 1939, and he kept the figure moving up until he signed for a near-record $90,000 a decade later. In addition, the Yankees had developed the habit of winning numerous pennants, so Joe was also being enriched by World Series checks.

He married actress Dorothy Arnold in 1939 and they had a son, Joe, Jr., who was born in October, 1941. Little Joe in later years was seen around the New York dugout, attired in a tiny Yankee uniform and proudly displaying a small-sized replica of his dad's glove.

Continuing his high-grade play, DiMaggio won the batting championship in 1939 and 1940. And in 1941 he put together his famous streak in which he hit safely in 56 consecutive games. When you consider that the previous record was 44 by Willie Keeler in

1897, you can see why this created such a stir. Joe had a couple of close calls before finally going hitless. In a game with St. Louis, he went into the ninth inning without a hit. He was the fourth scheduled batter, and when the first two men were retired it looked as though he might not get another time at bat. But Tommy Henrich bunted a three-and-one pitch and beat it out. Given one last chance, DiMaggio slammed a double to left and kept his streak intact.

On another occasion, Johnny Babich of the Athletics walked him the first time up and gave him three straight balls on his second appearance at the plate. Joe feared that Johnny never would give him anything he could hit, so he leaned across the plate for an outside pitch and slammed a single through the pitcher's box.

The streak finally came to an end in a night game at Cleveland, but it took superfielding by the Indians' Ken Keltner to do it. Twice Ken dove into the dirt around third base to dig up vicious drives and hurl DiMaggio out at first.

Joe's hits went for extra bases as often as not. For example, during a May 6 game with the Chicago White Sox at the Stadium, Joe hit a homer in the third. Then with the Yanks trailing, 5–4, he led off the ninth with one of his familiar triples. Joe Gordon followed with another three-base blast, and DiMaggio scored the tying run.

With the winning run on third, Thornton Lee, Chicago's pitcher, passed Bill Dickey and Frank

Crosetti intentionally to set up a force play at home. The strategy promptly backfired when John Sturm hit a short single to center that scored Gordon and ended the game.

On the strength of this robust batting and competent pitching, the Yankees rolled into another World Series. Their opponents were the Brooklyn Dodgers. Although the Yanks won in five games, there were a few high moments.

DiMaggio showed anger on the field of play for one of the very few times in his career. During the fifth game, Joe drove a long fly to center field, where it was finally captured by Pete Reiser. DiMaggio, who was almost at second base when the ball was caught, cut back near the pitcher's box on his way to the bench. Dodger hurler Whit Wyatt made some disparaging remark, which naturally couldn't be heard from the stands. DiMaggio turned on him swiftly, but players and umpires broke up the impending fracas before it started.

The big incident of the 1941 World Series, however, was Mickey Owen's unfortunate error. The Dodgers were leading, and the Yanks had two men out in the ninth. Tommy Henrich was the batter and he had two strikes. When he swung and missed the next pitch, it should have ended the game with the Dodgers victorious. But Owen, one of the most able catchers in the game, dropped the ball and Henrich scampered to first. The Yanks then strung together a couple of hits and won the game.

Although his average slipped to .305 in 1942, Joe knocked in 114 runs as the Yankees won another pennant. They clinched it September 14 at Cleveland. All Joe did was hit a homer and two singles, and save the game with an amazing catch in the ninth inning.

Center field at the Stadium didn't look natural for the next three years. Joe DiMaggio wasn't there. He enlisted in the Army Air Forces in February, 1943, and spent almost three years in the service. He came out a staff sergeant.

Opening Day, 1946, at Yankee Stadium, Joe got a welcome he'll probably never forget. His first time at bat, after a three-year absence, was the signal for a roar of whistles and cheers from the vast throng. Joe acknowledged the salute by tipping his hat and smashing a double to left off Washington's Mickey Haefner. He hit safely again in the seventh, but the Senators put on a rally and all but stole the game. They led, 6–5, going into the last of the ninth. Joe Gordon struck out, but George Stirnweiss walked and Henrich was hit by a pitched ball. Up stepped Joe DiMaggio, and he clipped another double down the left-field line, tying the score and placing the winning tally on third. It came in a minute later on a fly to center.

This was a fine start, but Joe's timing was still not sharp, and he ran into a serious slump during the middle of the season. He began to come out of it in August and pulled his average up to .290. It was the first time he had fallen below .300.

YANKEE CLIPPER

In 1947, he hit .315 and led the Yankees to the pennant. Their World Series adversaries were the Brooklyn Dodgers again, and out of one of the worst-played classics of all time Joe emerged as the real pro. There were errors, unexplainable base running, wild pitches, and 68 bases on balls—a World Series record. But despite this general loose play, it was a thoroughly exciting Series, with the Yankees winning in seven games. Through it all, DiMaggio stood out as the polished veteran, the finished ball player. He alone seemed to know what to do with the ball, where to make the play and how to do it. He provided the steadying influence and the leadership that took a below-average New York team to the world championship.

It was more this team spirit than an impressive set of records that brought him the Most Valuable Player award for the third time. Joe had proved himself a game and courageous ball player. He was never in the best physical condition; he had trouble with his throwing arm and later with a spur on his heel. But he managed to get out there almost every day and play winning ball.

Injuries plagued him through 1948, too, but he took part in 153 games as the Yanks lost a hectic race with the Cleveland Indians and Boston Red Sox. Joe hit .320 and led the league in homers with 39. Three of those four-base blows came in one game, and they indicate clearly how much DiMaggio meant to the Yankee team.

This was on May 23 at Cleveland, and one of the largest crowds ever to see a major-league game (78,431) jammed Municipal Stadium to watch the pennant contenders. The Yanks won the game, 6–5, with Joe knocking in every one of their runs. Cleveland was leading, 4–0, when Joe came up in the fourth with one on. He had already hit Bob Feller for a harmless single. Now he slammed a home run and made it 4–2. In the sixth inning, again facing the great Feller, he hit another, with two men on base. This put the Yanks in front, 5–4; but DiMaggio was still going strong. He hit No. 3 for the day in the eighth off Bob Muncrief. It's fortunate that he did hit this one, for the Indians had the tying run on third in the last of the ninth when Joe Page struck out Eddie Robinson for the final out.

Unlike most American League batters, Joe seemed to have considerable success with Bob Feller. There was another game when he hit him for a triple, a single, and a home run. The last-named blow came in the ninth inning with the score tied at 1–1 and won the game.

In deference to Feller, however, it must be admitted that the best pitchers in the game had trouble when Joe DiMaggio came up. He was at his best in the pinches. When a game hung in the balance, he was the man to step in and tip the scales. Not always with his bat, either: one day, running on a foot that probably caused him pain with every step, he dashed all the way back to the flagpole to pull down a tremendous drive and save a ball game. It was the ninth inning. There were two out and the bases full; the runners were on the move. If Joe had dropped the ball, three runs would have scored. But then, he never dropped it—at least, hardly ever.

Injuries plagued DiMaggio in his later years. At one time his throwing arm was so sore that he could make only one good peg a day from the outfield. Just at the end of the pre-game practice session he would let one go from deep center all the way in to the plate. That was it for the day. But opposition players and coaches, watching that throw, would mutter: "DiMaggio's arm must be okay. We won't be able to run on him today." Sometimes the ruse worked.

The great Yankee retired after the 1951 World Series and was voted into the Hall of Fame in 1955. He richly deserved the honor. Baseball fans will never forget "Jolting Joe" DiMaggio.

A Pair of Aces: Stan Musial and Ted Williams

Throughout the 1940's and 1950's you could always start an argument if you claimed that Stan Musial was a better ball player than Ted Williams, or vice versa. We won't try to settle the argument here. Both men were great, and any manager would have been happy to have either in his line-up. There are, however, some interesting comparisons to be made.

Each was the outstanding hitter in his league. There, possibly, the similarity stops; for these two men were completely different personalities on and off the field. Williams was moody and temperamental when he wasn't getting his base hits, but Musial appeared calm and easygoing no matter what the circumstances. On the other hand, Williams was the more spectacular and colorful, and undoubtedly drew more fans into more parks than did the quietly efficient Musial.

Perhaps Williams, the Boston Red Sox slugger, hit a ball harder than did Stan Musial of the St. Louis Cardinals—but not oftener. Nevertheless, there was something magnetic about Ted Williams when he stepped to the plate. People stopped eating peanuts, put down the bottle of pop. They concentrated on the action—Williams was up!

Lean and tall, he stood in the batter's box waving a bat savagely with sharp, full swings. When the pitch came up to the plate, he would uncoil his lanky frame with astonishing speed and lash the ball. The result, as often as not, would be an unbelievably hard line drive. It might go into the stands, or up against the fence—or directly into the hands of an outfielder. In any case, it would be a very hard-hit ball. He didn't, as a rule, hit the long, high fly as much as Babe Ruth. Williams' hits were rattling line drives. That's not to say he didn't hit plenty of homers, but when he did, the ball went into the stands or over the wall like a shot out of a cannon. He had terrific power and he was fascinating to watch. Blessed with extraordinarily good vision, he was seldom completely fooled by a pitch. If it was in there, he was almost sure to get at least a foul. Since he stubbornly refused to swing on a ball that was the least bit outside the strike zone, he received many bases on balls. Of course, this was frequently an intentional bit of strategy on the part of a harassed pitcher who would rather put him on first than take a chance on an extra-base hit.

Stanley Musial was no less feared in the National League than Williams was in the American. The St. Louis Cardinal ace would crouch at the plate with his bat far back. He seemed to be peeping over his shoulder at the pitcher. Then he would snap at the ball and line it over second or down the right-field line. Or maybe he would bunt, because he was very fast. He could hit the long ball, too, although not with the consistency over the years of Ted Williams. One of Stan's most famous long shots came in the 1948 All-Star game. It was the very first inning, two were out, and Richie Ashburn, the Phillies' fine rookie, was on first base. Stan "peeped" at Walt Masterson, of the Washington Senators, and then slashed the ball into the right-field stands, giving the Nationals a quick two-run lead. The fact that his team finally lost the game, 5–2, was hardly the fault of Mr. Musial. And although 1948 was only his sixth year in the big leagues, it marked the fifth time he had been chosen to play in the All-Star game.

A great team man and a great clutch hitter, Stan belonged on anybody's All-Star team. He was always at or near the top in runs batted in and total hits, led the league in batting on seven different occasions, and three times was named Most Valuable Player in the National League. He was a top-notch performer in every way. When the Cards needed a first baseman, he moved in from the outfield and played a fine game. Then he moved back to the outfield and picked up right where he left off. There was almost nothing the man couldn't do on the diamond. In fact, he started his baseball career as a pitcher, and it wouldn't have been too surprising to see him come racing in to the mound to take over the St. Louis hurling in a dangerous ninth inning.

"Stan Musial," said one National League manager during the 1948 season, "is the best left fielder, the best center fielder, the best right fielder, and the best first baseman in the league."

Williams was more of a specialist. A real superhitter, he was interested only in batting and cared little or nothing for the finer points of fielding. "I'm not running into any walls," he was quoted as saying. "I'll make a good try, but that's enough." Of course, he didn't mean that literally, and he made some fine plays in important games. But his forte was hitting, and on that he concentrated to the exclusion of almost everything else.

Most of his heroics on the diamond have already been recorded in detail, but let's take a quick look at a few of them again. There was the 1941 All-Star game in Detroit. The jubilant National Leaguers held a two-run lead going into the last half of the ninth inning. Then something happened. Singles by Kenny Keltner and Joe Gordon and a pass to Cecil Travis filled the bases with one out. Joe DiMaggio forced Travis at second, and Keltner scored. The Americans trailed by only one run, but there were two out. The batter was Williams. Pitcher Claude Passeau worked carefully—he was one out away from victory. So near and yet so far! Williams wheeled on the third pitch and sent a screaming drive into the right-field stands. He galloped gaily across the plate with the run that made it 7–5 in favor of the American League.

There was another All-Star game in which Williams ran the opposition into the ground. In the 1946 game at Fenway Park in Boston, he hammered out two homers and two singles as the National League was trounced 12–0. Bostonians will be talking about that second homer for a long time to come. Rip Sewell, of Pittsburgh, was on the hill and served up his famous "ephus" or "blooper" ball. This odd pitch would sail far up into the air and then drop down across the plate. It was a freak delivery, but Sewell had had some success with it in the National League. Most of the time batters swung and missed. Even if they did succeed in hitting the ball they couldn't seem to drive it anywhere. Williams watched the ball closely, timed it just right, and whacked it high into the stands. The Boston fans were delighted. So was Ted.

Williams had many big days. In 1946 the Red Sox were rolling to an American League pennant, but they ran into a last-minute slump and couldn't seem to win the one game that would clinch the flag. One day in Cleveland, Ted stepped up to the plate and found the infield and outfield shifted to the right as usual. It was the "Boudreau Shift," of course, designed especially for Williams. But this time Ted fooled the cagey Cleveland manager. He shifted his feet at the last second and blasted the ball into left field—where he wasn't supposed to be able to hit! The left fielder, way out of position, galloped in desperate pursuit. Williams, however, stretched his long legs and raced all the way around the bases for an inside-the-park homer that meant the pennant for Boston. That four-base belt, No. 38 of the season for Ted, probably gave him as much satisfaction as any he ever hit.

Williams, who gained such colorful nicknames as "the Splendid Splinter," "Terrible Ted," and "the Kid," was born in San Diego, California, on October 30, 1918, the son of Sam and May Williams. His father was in the photography business, and his mother was well known as an energetic worker for the Salvation Army.

Ted's first boyhood idol was the old Bambino himself. And like Babe Ruth, he started his baseball career as a pitcher and part-time outfielder. But no matter what position he was holding down in the field, he was terrific when he stepped into the batter's box.

He played so well and hit so hard that he attracted the attention of a New York Yankee scout. Somehow or other he escaped the Yankee farm chain and was signed by San Diego, of the Pacific Coast League. He was only seventeen years old at the time, but he hammered PCL pitching with such lusty abandon that the next year he was sold to the Boston Red Sox.

Ted Williams reported to the big-league camp in the spring of 1938. He was said to have been a very fresh rookie. When his friend Bobby Doerr remarked, "Boy! Wait till you see this Foxx [Jimmy] hit!" Ted replied, "Hah! Wait till Foxx sees me!"

Although he showed more promise than most youngsters, he was sent to Minneapolis, in the minors, for further seasoning. He had a grand year and smashed out 43 home runs in the process of compiling a .366 batting average.

He wasn't the easiest player in the world to handle in those days. They tell the story of the time he came snarling back to the bench after failing to get a hit. He was in such a rage that he took his bat and smashed the water cooler to pieces.

Another amusing Williams anecdote: Once he woke up in the middle of the night and started practicing his swing in front of the mirror in his hotel room. He misjudged one of these practice swings and hit the bed in which his roommate was sleeping. The bed went down with a crash, dumping his surprised teammate on the floor. "Gosh!" said Williams, surveying the destruction. "What power!"

Back with the Red Sox in 1939, he showed little respect for big-league pitching. He hit .321 and picked up 31 home runs. Small wonder that he was named Rookie of the Year. He was even better the next year with .344; but he hit his peak in 1941. That was the year he topped everybody with a wondrous .406. It was the first time an American Leaguer had been over .400 since Harry Heilmann's great 1923 season.

Ted had to break out in a rash of base hits on the last day of the season to get over the magic figure. The Red Sox were in Philadelphia for a doubleheader, and Ted was hitting almost an even .400. Legend has it that manager Joe Cronin told him he could have the day off, thus preserving his near-.400 average. "No!" snapped Williams. "I'll make it anyway!"

Williams stepped up to the plate eight times on that last day and lined out six safe hits. That took care of the batting average, and it also indicates the confidence the great slugger had in himself.

In 1942, he was again the league's ace hitter with a .356 figure and 38 home runs. That was all the baseball for Ted for a while. There was a war on, and Williams enlisted as a cadet in the Navy Air Corps. He spent most of the next three years in the service, and set a record for accuracy in shooting at a target from a plane. They say that when he was given his physical examination, doctors were amazed at his wonderful eyesight and reported that Ted could see almost twice as well as a normal person. American

League pitchers were only mildly surprised at this news—they had suspected something of the sort for a long time.

Back in Boston in 1946, Ted powered the Red Sox into a World Series date with the St. Louis Cardinals. He hit .342, drove in 123 runs, and walloped 38 homers.

The Series itself was a seven-game thriller for the fans, but it was just a big and painful headache to Ted Williams. The most publicized hitter in the game was held to five hits by the clever Cardinal pitchers. He hit an even .200 and was probably the most disappointed man who ever took part in the annual classic. His opposite number, Stan Musial, didn't do much better, gathering only six hits for .222. But all eyes were on Williams, and the fans weren't the least bit shy about letting the Boston slugger know what they thought of his performance.

It's an odd fact that despite his spectacular achievements, Williams was far from popular with the majority of the fans. Perhaps it was because from the stands he appeared to be a sullen, brooding man, especially when things weren't going too smoothly. Maybe, too, it was his lackadaisical attitude toward the business of fielding. Once, in a game at Yankee Stadium, Ted was called out on strikes—a most unusual event—and was still sulking when he took his place in left field. You could see him out there kicking the ground and talking to himself, still thinking about that decision. Just then a Yankee batter slammed a long, high fly to left. Williams looked up and lost the ball in the sun—he had been so upset he had forgotten to put on his sun glasses. The ball went for two bases and scored a New York run. The Yankees won the game by just that margin.

But if Ted lost that one, he made up for it many times over with his long, hard blows in the clutch. Pitchers were in trouble when Williams stepped up to the plate. As one knowing American League hurler put it: "The thing to do is work hard on the batters preceding Williams. If you get him up there with the bases empty, he can't hurt you too much even if he does hit it out of the park."

In his first year in the majors, Ted hit at Detroit one of the longest homers ever recorded. The ball is said to have traveled over 500 feet; it sailed over the double-decked stands in right field. It must have been a terrific belt. But there were so many sensational Williams homers that it was hard to keep track of them. One day he hit three in a single game, the first of a double-header against the Cleveland Indians. It was between games that Lou Boudreau designed the famous shift that was to plague Ted from then on. But as other teams adopted the shift, Ted learned to hit to left field. He made some 70 hits in that direction in 1948, thus minimizing to some degree the effectiveness of the weird defensive maneuver.

As the Red Sox came within an eyelash of the 1948 pennant, Williams had one of his best years. With .369, he led his league for the fourth time. Only two other American League batters—Ty Cobb and Harry Heilmann—had won four batting crowns.

One of Ted's most successful days in 1948 came on June 11, when he pounded in seven runs as the Red Sox walked over the Chicago White Sox, 12–4. Ted hit two doubles and a single, and each time he sent two runners scurrying across the plate. Finally he came up with the bases full, and Orval Grove, Chicago's disgusted hurler, adopted a desperate measure and gave him a base on balls. This forced in one run, of course, but apparently it was better than letting Williams hit again.

Five days later at Cleveland, Ted took charge of Bob Feller himself. As Boston bombarded the Indians, 7–4, Williams contributed a home run, two doubles, and a single, and gathered another base on balls.

It obviously wasn't Ted's fault that the Red Sox didn't crash into the World Series. He gave the team everything he had. He did it again in 1949, when he won the Most Valuable Player award. That was the year he socked 43 home runs, knocked in 159 runs, and hit for a solid average of .343.

Baseball was so important to him that he made it a point to keep in good condition all year round. Next to batting in a ball game, his favorite occupation was fishing. Occasionally he would disappear into the wilderness and not show up for a week or more. But by the time spring came around, he was always eager to start swinging a bat.

A PAIR OF ACES

Williams was called back into the service again in 1952 and flew jet planes through the skies of Korea. When he returned after fifteen months, it was feared that his baseball days might well be numbered. He was almost thirty-six at the time. But after working out for a few weeks, with occasional pinch-hitting roles, he was ready for steady duty. And amazingly enough, he seemed just as good as ever. In his first game he belted a home run and a double. And three days later, he beat the Philadelphia Athletics with a late-inning two-run home run. American League pitchers shook their heads in despair—it was the same Terrible Ted.

Stan Musial, possibly the best left-handed hitter in National League history, was born November 21, 1920, in the small town of Donora in western Pennsylvania. He was one of six children, the son of a steel worker.

A flashy forward on the basketball team, Stan was awarded a place in the All-Western Pennsylvania High School aggregation. As a result, he was offered a scholarship at several colleges. But, overcoming strong parental objections, Stan took a baseball job with Williamson of the Mountain State League. He began his career as a pitcher. By 1940 he was with Daytona Beach in the Florida State (Class D) League. There he won fifteen and lost five. He was also developing into a fine hitter, and his manager, Dick Kerr, occasionally put him in the Daytona outfield.

One day while he was taking care of his outfield chores, he tried to make a shoestring catch and fell on his left shoulder. That wound up his career as a pitcher and almost finished him as a baseball player.

The story goes that he was discouraged and ready to go back home to Donora, but Kerr persuaded him to stick with the game. "After all," Dick argued, "you can still hit!"

He was a busy young man in 1941. He played 87 games for Springfield, 54 for Rochester, and 12 for St. Louis. When he arrived in the big leagues, his team, the Cardinals, was involved in a hot pennant fight with the Brooklyn Dodgers. Although the Cards failed to overtake the Brooklyn entry, the playing of their rookie outfielder was more than surprising. In his 12 games, Musial murdered opposition hurling for a .426 average. Few first-year men get off to such a jet-propelled start.

His steady .315 hitting and alert play in the outfield helped the Cardinals to a National League pennant in 1942. Although Yankee pitchers held his bat in check in the Series, the Cardinals—running and fielding to beat the band—upset the New Yorkers and won the championship. The third game was typical. Stan, Terry Moore, and Enos Slaughter drove the Yankees crazy as they raced to all corners of the Stadium to pick off what looked like sure hits. Ernie White won the game, 2–0, but he certainly owed a vote of thanks to his wonderful outfield.

Musial really hit his stride in 1943 when he led the

A PAIR OF ACES

league with a .357 mark. He was the top man in total hits, doubles, and triples and was named Most Valuable Player in the National circuit. All this is rather amazing when you consider that he was only a twenty-two-year-old who had wanted to quit the game three years before.

The year 1944 was another good one for "the Donora Greyhound," but his .347 wasn't good enough to retain the batting crown. He lost it to Brooklyn's Dixie Walker as the Dodger veteran came up with a .357 mark. Musial, playing in a World Series for the third straight year, hit a homer, two doubles, and four singles as the Cards beat the Browns in the first all-St. Louis clash.

After a year in the U.S. Navy, Stan came back in 1946 apparently as skillful as ever. He proved his versatility when he was called on to play first base because of an injury to the regular first sacker. After a few games, he looked as though he had been playing that position all his life. His .365 made him the National League's hitting champion and shoved the Cardinals into another pennant. But they had to do it the hard way, via a play-off series with their old friends the Dodgers.

Each team finished the regular season with 96 won and 58 lost. The first game of the play-off series took place in St. Louis, and the home team, with left-hander Howie Pollet having one of his better days, trimmed the Dodgers, 4–2. Musial had only one hit, but it was a triple. He scored twice. The teams went to Brooklyn the next day, and St. Louis ended the long season with a one-sided 8–4 victory.

The fast-moving Cards kept right on going and took the Red Sox into camp in the World Series. This was a seven-game duel, and in the final analysis it was again Cardinal speed, plus the superhurling of Harry ("the Cat") Brecheen, who won three games, that made the difference. Enos Slaughter's dash for the plate in the eighth inning of the last game provided the winning touch. Enos stood on first, with two out, when Harry Walker lined a savage hit over second. The fleet Slaughter raced for third and, as Boston's Johnny Pesky hesitated momentarily in handling the relay from the outfield, sailed on into the plate. That was the winning run, scored in typical Cardinal fashion.

A troublesome appendix got Musial off to a slow start in 1947. As a result, the Cardinals got off to a slow start, too. By the middle of June the champs were struggling to escape from the basement, and their great slugger was hitting around .200.

But baseball's famous physician Dr. Robert Francis Hyland, of St. Louis, patched up Stan and made it possible for him to finish the season without an operation. Musial got going in July, and from there to the finish he and the Cardinals were extremely dangerous. By hitting at a .400 clip for the last month or so, Musial dragged his average up to .312 and the Cardinals up to second place.

During the off-season, Stan had his appendix

A PAIR OF ACES

removed. The enforced inactivity at that time of the year didn't bother him. He was accustomed to living quietly with his family. He was strictly the domestic type. He married his boyhood sweetheart, Lillian Labash, while he was still in the minors, and they had two children, Richard and Geraldine.

Musial had his greatest year in 1948. Few men have ever had better ones. He was a nightmare to National League hurlers, and he tied a record set by Ty Cobb when he got five hits in one game on four different occasions. He picked on good pitchers, too. Twice it was the staff of the pennant-winning Boston Braves that was hammered.

Stan started on April 30 against Cincinnati with a homer, two doubles, and two singles. On May 19 at Brooklyn he had a triple, two doubles, and two singles. Incidentally, he also scored five runs in this game. On June 22, at Boston, he rapped out five successive singles; later he went back to Boston again and hit a homer, a double, and three singles.

This was cannonading the like of which the National League hadn't seen since the heyday of Rogers Hornsby. Stanley, who was handed the Most Valuable Player award for the third time, led his league in all hitting departments save one. He had the highest average, scored the most runs, had the most hits, most doubles, most triples, most total bases, and the highest slugging percentage. The only honor he missed on was the homer title. He hit 39, trailing Johnny Mize and Ralph Kiner, who tied at 40.

At the conclusion of this exciting season, Stan signed a two-year contract calling for approximately $50,000 a year, big money in those days. Although this figure falls considerably below that paid such performers as Ruth, Feller, Williams, and DiMaggio, still it is said to have been the highest salary ever paid by the Cardinal organization. And it was destined to go even higher.

Williams and Musial were two of the greatest the old game has ever seen. They continued their terrific play through the late 1950's. On May 13, 1958, Musial slammed out a double to win a game. It was his 3,000th base hit; at that time only seven men had accomplished this feat in the history of the game.

Williams, too, was setting all-time records. In 1957 he led the American League in batting for the fifth time. He was the oldest player in history to win a batting crown, and he was named Top American League Player by *The Sporting News.* Both men had great years in 1958. Williams won another batting title—his sixth—with .328. And Musial finished third in the National League with a resounding .337.

Only time could stop Ted and Stan. Williams called it a career after the 1960 season. Late that year he socked one into the stands, trotted around the bases, and disappeared into the dugout. The next day he announced his retirement. "Stan the Man" battled on through 1961 on a part-time basis, still delivering those line-drive singles and doubles when they were needed. He was a tough man to get out—any way you looked at it. And every time he got a hit he broke a record.

The Pride of Milwaukee: Warren Spahn

The unsung hero of Milwaukee's sensational rise to the championship of the baseball world, just five years after the club was moved from Boston, was a quiet, gaunt, angular left-handed pitcher who was actually one of the greatest hurlers the National League had ever seen.

Yet oddly enough, people don't seem to know much about Warren Spahn. He was not a headline hunter; he didn't make trouble; he didn't fight with umpires or other players. He was just a pleasant,

THE PRIDE OF MILWAUKEE

polite man with a serious attitude toward baseball—and a wonderful talent for pitching.

In the fall of 1957 his teammate Lew Burdette beat the New York Yankees three times in the World Series, twice shutting them out. It was a wonderful feat, and was so acclaimed all over the nation. But fans seemed to forget that without quiet Warren Spahn, the Milwaukee Braves never would have been in the Series.

The next year, on September 13, 1958, Spahn beat the St. Louis Cardinals 8–2 and clinched the pennant for the Braves. On that date he also became the first left-hander in major-league history to record nine 20-game seasons. Four more of these 20-game seasons followed for the classy lefty. His lifetime record when he retired in 1965 at age forty-four was 363 victories against 245 defeats, with an earned-run average of 3.08. Like a real champion, he was at his best in the clutch. Said one of the Brave coaches: "If there's one game you just have to win, then you must go with Spahn. He's got the heart."

Spahn achieved his great records despite some of the worst luck a pitcher ever ran into. For a time it seemed that the Braves could not score a run when Warren was on the mound. As a result, he lost innumerable well-pitched games by scores of 1–0, 2–1, 3–1.

In one four-day stretch in 1952 he lost two 3–1 games, to Chicago and Cincinnati. But look at the way the man was pitching!

The game with the Cubs went fifteen innings. Warren pitched every one of them and struck out eighteen men. Furthermore the Braves were leading going into the ninth inning because of a home run which Spahn himself hit. The Cubs tied the score in the ninth and beat him in the fifteenth when he gave up two bases on balls—his only passes in the entire game. Meanwhile his own teammates had come up with exactly four hits.

Three days later the tireless lefty was back on the hill against the Cincinnati Redlegs. This time the Braves contrived to get seven hits and one run for him. That meant that in 24 innings the Braves had scored two runs, and Spahn's homer was one of them. Warren grinned ruefully and struck out eleven of the Redleg batters to establish a record for one pitcher in two successive games.

But he never complained. Once he dropped a 1–0 decision when his center fielder, Johnny Hopp, misjudged a fly. It went over his head for a triple and scored a run. After the game Warren walked over to Hopp's locker. "Forget it, Johnny," he said to the downcast youngster. "If we hadn't lost it one way we'd have done it another."

Of course, he won many great ones, too. Strangely, one of the games he's most proud of was a relief job. It was in the 1948 World Series against the Cleveland Indians. Spahn had lost the second game when, as usual, the Braves got just one run. Now it was the

THE PRIDE OF MILWAUKEE 159

fifth game, and the Indians put on a storm against Nelson Potter and drove him from the box in the fourth inning to take a 5-4 lead.

In to pitch for the National Leaguers came Warren Spahn. He relieved Potter with one out in the fourth inning and slammed the door on the Indians. In five and two-thirds innings he gave no runs, one little hit, and one base on balls. He was tremendous. Lou Boudreau, manager of the Cleveland club, said, "This was one of the finest pieces of clutch pitching I've ever seen."

Something else happened that day to make Warren happy. His mates got him some runs. They staged a six-run rally in the seventh, and the Braves won the game 11-5.

Warren Edward Spahn was born April 23, 1921, in Buffalo, New York. His father, Edward Spahn, was a wallpaper salesman and a semi-pro ball player.

Young Warren started out as a first baseman. By the time he was nine years old he was playing for the midget team of the Lake City Athletic Club, while his father was playing third for the senior team. A few years later there was one wonderful season when father and son were playing in the same infield.

His pitching career started when he entered South Park High School. The team had an All-Scholastic first baseman, and Warren didn't figure he could beat him out for the job. So he turned to pitching—quite a sensible move, as it turned out. He was so successful that the Boston Braves became interested and sent a scout to look him over. The scout liked what he saw, and Warren signed with the Braves organization.

He was sent to Bradford, Pennsylvania, in the Pony League, and had nothing but tough luck. He injured his pitching arm twice and actually worked only 66 innings. He was afraid his career was over—at the age of nineteen!

But his arm regained its resiliency, and with Evansville, Indiana, in the Three-Eye League he won nineteen games and lost six in 1941. The Braves thought he was almost ready for the major leagues but finally decided to give him one more year of seasoning. He promptly won seventeen games for Hartford, of the Eastern League, and was brought up to Boston at the end of the season.

The country was now at war, and Warren was called into the Armed Forces. He had an extraordinary military record. He was in the European Theater for a year and a half and was in almost constant action. Attached to the 276th Combat Engineers Battalion, he was right in the middle of the Battle of the Bulge and had another rough time at the Remagen bridgehead. He was wounded once—in the foot. He received the Bronze Star and a Purple Heart. He was quite a soldier.

When he got back to the States in 1946, there were two reception committees waiting. One was composed of Miss Lorene Southard, of Tulsa, Oklahoma, whom he had met before he went overseas and planned to marry when he got back. The other committee was composed of the entire Boston Braves organization, who were badly in need of a good left-handed pitcher. Warren and Lorene wanted to get married right away. The Braves wanted them to wait until the season was over. Finally after much discussion they got married in August. But it was obviously hard for Warren to concentrate on baseball, and the record shows it: he won eight and lost five.

The Braves were building now and coming up with some fine young players. They finished third in 1947, and Spahn, now the ace of the staff, won 21 and lost 10 while fanning 123. And his sparkling 2.33 earned-run average topped the league.

Warren was slow getting started in 1948, but he came on like the wind at the finish. It was Spahn and the good right-hander Johnny Sain who finally brought a pennant to Boston. In mid-August manager Billy Southworth realized a championship was a definite possibility. But he had a problem—his pitching was weak except for Spahn and Sain. Southworth began working Warren and Johnny one after the other. To do this, he took every possible advantage of schedule breaks and bad weather. It was about this time that a Boston sportswriter coined the expression: "Spahn and Sain and pray for rain."

This will give you an idea of what these two men were doing: Spahn pitched the first game of the September 6 Labor Day double-header with the

Dodgers. It was a terrific pitchers' duel, but Warren came out on top after fourteen innings. The score was 2–1 and he allowed exactly five hits. Johnny Sain worked the second game, and when he came up with a 4–0 victory, the Braves were in front by four games. There were no games scheduled for the next two days—and then it rained! Spahn and Sain were ready to go again, and they beat the Philadelphia Phillies twice. There was another day off, and then two other members of the pitching staff got a split in a double-header. Sain and Spahn beat the Cubs on the 14th and 15th. There was no game scheduled for the next day, and then the same pair went back to work against the Pittsburgh Pirates. They both won—and it just about wound up the pennant race. But the two aces had worn themselves out, and they were edged in the World Series by the Cleveland Indians in six games.

The next four years were not happy ones for the Braves or their fans, who were becoming fewer each year. The Braves finished fourth for three straight years and came in a terrible seventh in 1952. However, it should be noted that their southpaw ace piled up no less than 78 victories in that period, making him the top pitcher in the National League. He led in strike-outs, and was always close to the top in innings pitched.

Probably Spahn's best pitch was a well-controlled fast ball, but he also had an excellent slow curve. When he wound up and stretched his long arms and kicked his right leg high, the batter felt he was seeing nothing but waving arms and legs—and the ball came out of nowhere.

In 1953, after that dismal seventh-place finish and years of losing money, the club owners moved the franchise to Milwaukee. This city was mad for major-league baseball, and it gave the Braves a royal reception and—even more important—packed the ball park. The players were astounded and delighted —Boston was never like this! They showed their appreciation by driving immediately into a contending position in the National League. The team that moved to Milwaukee was not as bad as its seventh-place finish would indicate, and, responding to the roaring cheers of the Milwaukee fans, the Braves fought for every game. They were second in '53, third in '54, second again in '55 and '56. Even though they lost the pennant in the last week of the 1956 season, they were regarded in many quarters as the best club in the league.

The Braves were really loaded with talent now. In addition to Spahn (Sain had been sold), the pitching staff numbered such aces as Lew Burdette, Bob Buhl, and Gene Conley. Red Schoendienst, Eddie Mathews, Joe Adcock, and Johnny Logan made a superb infield. Hank Aaron, Eddie Pafko, Wes Covington, and Bill Bruton gave them a strong, hard-hitting outfield squad.

It surprised practically no one when this wrecking crew brought Milwaukee its first pennant in 1957.

And the city went wild cheering its heroes as they moved into the World Series with the New York Yankees.

Spahn, who had won 21 games during the season, was Milwaukee's choice to open the Series in Yankee Stadium. He was opposed by Whitey Ford, lefty ace of the New Yorkers, who rendered the Braves powerless; they got but one run and five hits. The result: a tough 3–1 loss for Spahn. Burdette then won the first of his three games, and the show moved to Milwaukee. The Braves played a miserable game before their own fans and were walloped 12–3.

In the fourth tilt Warren Spahn hurled one of the grittiest games of his career. It was a thriller. Spahn's curve wasn't breaking as sharply as usual and he didn't seem to be quite as fast, but the Braves needed a victory. Despite numerous difficulties he held the hard-hitting Yankees to one run for eight innings, and by that time his mates had built a 4–1 lead. Warren had two men out in the ninth, and there were two Yanks on base; Elston Howard was the batter. The count went to three-and-two. Needing but one strike to end the game, Spahn fired his fast ball. It was too good—Howard hit it into the left-field stands for a home run that tied the score.

Nobody knows what Spahn was thinking. Victory, it appeared, had been snatched away from him at the very last second. But if he was disheartened, it didn't show. He got the third out, and watched his own team fail to score in the last of the ninth. The game went into the tenth inning, and the Yankees scored a run.

Now it was the last call for the Braves. Nippy Jones, a pinch hitter, was hit on the foot by a pitched ball and then sacrificed to second. Milwaukee fans came back to life with a roar when Johnny Logan doubled into the left-field corner, scoring Jones with the tying run; and they went out of their minds when, a minute later, Eddie Mathews slugged the ball over the right-field fence to win the game. It was a great victory—a real team effort. And the Braves went on from there to win the world championship.

The Braves were handicapped by injuries through much of the 1958 season, but this was a sound club, and it hammered its way to another National League pennant and a World Series date with the New York Yankees.

It was another good year for Spahn. When the great southpaw won his twentieth game on September 13, he broke a tie with two immortal American League left-handers, Lefty Grove and Eddie Plank, both of Philadelphia. They had each come through with eight 20-game seasons. For Warren this was the ninth time—and he won two more games before the season was over.

In the tense, dramatic Series with the Yankees, Warren was a heroic figure. Twice he defeated the New Yorkers, and he came close to doing it a third time. But the Yankees overcame a 3–1 deficit in games and went on to win—a remarkable performance.

Warren Spahn, however, was really coming into his own. He won 21 games in each of the next three years and became the winningest southpaw in history. In 1973 he was elected to the Baseball Hall of Fame by a landslide vote of the Baseball Writers Association of America. "This," said Spahn, "was the greatest victory of my life."

Pioneer on the Base Paths: Jackie Robinson

Baseball took a giant step forward on April 15, 1947, at Ebbets Field in Brooklyn. That was the day Jackie Robinson trotted down to first base for the Dodgers and became the first Negro to play in the major leagues. Many blacks followed him, and today are of course among the outstanding players in both leagues. But Jackie was the first—he broke the "color line."

It wasn't easy. On entering the big leagues, Robinson encountered intense hostility from fans, players on opposing teams, and even some of his own teammates. He had to face insults from crowds at ball parks all over the league. When he came to bat, some pitchers threw dangerously close to his head. When the Dodgers were on the road, he was barred from some hotels that were perfectly happy to house the white members of the team. But he survived in this atmosphere, even flourished. He was named Rookie of the Year in 1947, and received the Most Valuable Player award in 1949 when he hit a blazing .342. In ten years Jackie's speed and catlike grace on the field, his clutch hits, and his fiery aggressiveness carried the Dodgers to six pennants and Brooklyn's only world championship.

Perhaps his personality was revealed most clearly when he was on base. Six feet tall, weighing 195 pounds, Robinson ran with the speed and determination of an All-American halfback.

He seemed to come alive, almost to give off sparks, when he was on base. He once told a reporter that what he enjoyed most about baseball was his private war with the pitcher, who would be trying desperately to keep him from taking too much of a lead and heading for the next base.

"I think my value to the Dodgers," he said, "was disruption, making the pitcher concentrate on me instead of my teammate who was at bat." His tactics, picked up by other ball players, led to television's introduction of the split screen, which allows the viewer to watch both the runner on first and the pitcher on the mound. Jackie stole an average of 20 bases a year; he was a constant threat to go for an extra base on any kind of hit.

"The only way to beat the Dodgers," said Warren Giles, then president of the Cincinnati Reds, "is to keep Robinson off the bases."

Jackie Robinson was a fighter in addition to being a talented ball player. He fought for the right to play ball in the major leagues, and he also fought all his life to make his dreams of racial equality come true. He made history in a way that touched the common man—on the baseball diamond.

Jackie's entrance into the big leagues was engineered by that astute manipulator of men and teams, Branch Rickey, then president of the Dodgers. For three years he had his scouts looking at the Negro leagues for the right man to break the color line. Reports covered everything from a player's speed, stamina, and hitting ability to his personal habits and conduct off the field.

Rickey studied the reports carefully. He had to have the right man for his "noble experiment." One name kept coming up again and again.

Son of a sharecropper and grandson of a slave, Jack Roosevelt Robinson was born in Cairo, Georgia, on January 31, 1919, one of five children of Mallie and Jerry Robinson. Jackie was six months old when his father left the family. Soon after, his mother took the youngsters to her brother's home in Pasadena, California. Jack grew up in an atmosphere of sports and apparently excelled in every game he had time to play. He was so good that the youngsters in his neighborhood would bribe him with soft drinks to get him to play on their team.

"I was a pro at an early age," he remarked later.

He was surely an all-round athlete. At high school, Pasadena Junior College, and UCLA he won letters in baseball, football, track, and basketball.

Jackie left UCLA after two years, suddenly depressed at the lack of opportunities available to black men, even with a college degree. He also felt a pressing need to help support his mother. He joined a semi-pro football team, the Honolulu Bears. While he was on a ship heading home to Pasadena in December, 1941, bombs rained down on Pearl Harbor, and shortly thereafter Jack was drafted into the Army. While he was stationed at Fort Hood in Texas, he became embroiled with a bus driver who insisted that he move from the seat he occupied to one in the rear of the bus. Robinson refused, and faced court-martial charges stemming from the incident. He was ultimately acquitted of all charges.

When the war ended and Jackie returned to civilian life, he found himself in trouble. He had no college degree, no job, and no trade. To earn money, he decided to join a professional baseball team, the Kansas City Monarchs of the Negro National League. He was there when Dodger scout Clyde Sukeforth found him and told him Rickey wanted to see him in Brooklyn.

Rickey studied the young black man standing before him and knew he had the right subject for the experiment. The canny Rickey explained the problems the first Negro in the white man's baseball world would be up against. Robinson was tight-lipped, but he knew it was the big chance.

"The man for this job," said Rickey, "has to have the guts not to fight back." Robinson stared at him. Was the man looking for an "Uncle Tom"? Then he realized Rickey was looking for strength of a different sort, not weakness. "I have two cheeks," he said. "Is that what you want to hear?"

Jackie signed a contract and was assigned to Montreal, the Dodgers' No. 1 farm club, where he was an instant sensation at shortstop. The stage was set for the next step in Rickey's plan. Jackie was brought to Ebbets Field.

The going was rough. During spring training in 1947, a group of Dodger players signed a petition demanding Robinson's removal from the club. After the season started, the St. Louis Cardinals threatened to strike rather than play against him.

Through it all, Robinson performed brilliantly and won the battle to control his normal aggressive temperament. What's more, the malcontents on the Dodger team, realizing that this hard-fighting, hard-hitting rookie could literally put money in all their pockets, got behind him, and Brooklyn surged to a National League pennant. But waiting for them in the World Series were the all-conquering New York Yankees. The Brooklyn heroes struggled desperately, but the Yanks won it, four games to three. It had been a fine season, however, for Jackie, who was named the National League's Rookie of the Year.

A shortage of pitchers stopped the Dodgers in 1948, but they were back at the top again the following year. Robinson, now at second base, was tremendous as he slugged the ball for a .342 average and turned in one impossible fielding play after another. He easily won the National League's Most Valuable Player award.

Robinson was now an established star, and Rickey no longer encouraged him to restrain himself. Jackie began to reply outspokenly to the insults and criticisms he received.

He continued his brilliant and exciting play on the field. Although he hit for a modest .311 lifetime average, with 137 home runs, he batted cleanup on a team with such famous sluggers as Duke Snider, Gil Hodges, and Roy Campanella. It was a tribute to his ability to come up with a hit when teammates were on the bases.

Robinson was the type of player who refused to accept the very idea of defeat. In 1951 the Dodgers were engaged in a tense struggle with the New York Giants for the National League title. It was the last day of the season, and the teams were tied for first place. The Dodgers were playing in Philadelphia, and late in the afternoon they looked up on the scoreboard and saw: New York 3, Boston 2. Brooklyn had to win or "wait till next year."

The Phillies were giving the Dodgers a fierce

battle—the score was tied in the bottom of the twelfth inning. It was 6 P.M. and the light was failing, but league rules forbade turning on lights for a game starting at 2 o'clock. Red Smith, one of the country's top sports writers, tells what happened: "With two out and the bases full of Phillies, Eddie Waitkus smashes a low violent drive toward centerfield. The ball is a blur passing second base, difficult to follow in the half-light, impossible to catch. Jackie Robinson catches it. He flings himself headlong at right angles to the flight of the ball. For an instant his body is suspended in mid-air, then somehow the outstretched glove intercepts the ball inches off the ground. Robinson falls hard. But the Phillies are out and the score is still tied."

The game rumbled on into the fourteenth inning. It was too dark to play but they kept on anyway. In the Dodger half of the inning, Peewee Reese and Duke Snider popped out. Philadelphia pitcher Robin Roberts got a strike and a ball on Robinson. Jackie hit the next pitch high into the left-field stands. That was the clincher—and that was Jackie Robinson, who would not be defeated, whose desire drove him to reach the unreachable ball and eventually win the game.

Thus the season ended in a tie, and in a memorable play-off series, the Giants edged the Dodgers on Bobby Thomson's last-ditch storybook homer.

The next two years were frustrating ones for the Dodgers. Each time they won the National League pennant and then were beaten by the New York

Yankees in the World Series. But these were fine Yankee teams that were pushing the Dodgers around in the big fall classic. Manager Casey Stengel had put together an all-but-unbeatable combination of effective hitting and tremendous pitching. From 1949 through 1953 Stengel's club won five straight World Series—and on three occasions the Brooklyn Dodgers were the victims.

In the 1952 Series the Dodgers got off to a fine start when they beat the Yanks, 4–2, behind the excellent pitching of Joe Black and home runs by Robinson, Snider, and Reese. The next day the Yanks evened the tally with a 7–1 victory; but the Dodgers bounced back in the third game, 5–3, and led two games to one. But then the Yankees took charge, winning three of the next four and picking up all the marbles—four games to three.

Again in 1953 the Dodgers fell before the Yankees despite the valiant efforts of Jackie Robinson, who banged out eight hits for a .320 average, and pitcher Carl Erskine, who won the third game of the Series with a tremendous performance that included fourteen strike-outs. Brooklyn was undone by the twelve-hit assault of Yankee second sacker Billy Martin. Throughout the Series, Martin played a mile over his head—a fact duly recorded by Brooklyn manager Charlie Dressen. "We were beaten by a .250 hitter," he moaned.

In 1954 the Dodgers were trounced by their old National League rivals the New York Giants, who had acquired an ace left-handed pitcher, Johnny Antonelli, from the Milwaukee Braves and who benefited from the services of superstar Willie Mays, back from the Army. The Giants were just too tough for the rest of the league.

The slugging of Robinson, Snider, Hodges, and Campanella brought joy to Brooklyn and powered the club back to the top in 1955. And that meant another World Series date with the powerful Yankees. Would this be the year to end the domination of the hated intruders from across the river? Brooklyn fans were sure it was—but then, they were always optimistic.

The Flatbush faithful were sunk in despair, however, when the Yankees swept through the first two games in Yankee Stadium, 6–5 and 4–2. Back in Ebbets Field the Brooklyn batting order suddenly came alive, and the Dodgers ripped the Yanks in three straight games. Returning to the Stadium, the Yankees rallied to win the sixth game—but Johnny Podres hurled the Dodgers to victory in the finale, 2–0, and Brooklyn had its first world championship. It turned out to be the only one, for two years later the Dodgers left Brooklyn for Los Angeles.

Although he didn't have a great Series, Jackie Robinson did manage a steal of home in the first game, a rare feat at any time but especially in a World Series. In his lifetime Jackie stole home eleven times, more than any other player in the post-World War II era.

Jackie had married early in his career, and now he and his wife, Rachel, had three children: Jack, Jr.; Sharon; and David. In fact Rachel and young Jack, then four and a half months old, were in the stands that memorable day in 1947 when Jackie took the field for the first time for the Dodgers.

In 1956 Robinson was thirty-seven, and nearing the end of his exciting big-league career. Before retiring, however, he led the Dodgers to one more pennant. And again, for the sixth time in Jackie's ten years, the Yankees were waiting for him in the World Series. It was just the reverse of the previous year, with the Dodgers getting the first two games, the Yanks the next three, and the teams splitting the last two. It was another Yankee victory, of course, four games to three.

The turning point came in the fifth game with the clubs tied at two games apiece. Don Larsen, an erratic Yankee right-hander, picked this particular time to come up with the first perfect game in World Series history. He retired the Dodgers one-two-three for nine straight innings as he wrote his name in red letters in the record books. Jackie Robinson almost upset the apple cart for him as early as the second inning, when he drove a wicked smash to the right of third base. Although Andy Carey, the Yankees' good third baseman, got a glove on it, the ball bounced past. But it took just the right bounce for shortstop Gil McDougald to grab it on the hop and fire to first, getting the fast Robinson by an eyelash. That was as close as the Dodgers came to giving Larsen any trouble.

It was Jackie Robinson's last year in baseball. Off the diamond, he continued his fight for the black man's right to equal opportunity in other areas of life. He was involved in the founding of Freedom National Bank, a New York bank owned and operated by blacks; and he headed the Jackie Robinson Land Development Corporation in New York, which built multifamily dwellings for blacks, largely in minority communities.

Later he was appointed Special Assistant to Governor Nelson Rockefeller of New York and became a forthright critic of the government's lack of attention to the problems of the black community.

On January 23, 1962, Robinson became the first black man elected to baseball's Hall of Fame, an honor he richly deserved and of which he was deeply proud.

Heart-breaking tragedy entered Robinson's life when his eldest boy, Jack, Jr., became a drug addict. The young man beat the heroin habit, then died at twenty-four in an automobile accident. He had been "clean" for three years.

Jack's health began to fail him in his early fifties. He survived one heart attack, contracted diabetes and high blood pressure, and was going blind.

Right to the end he pushed his demand for racial equality. At a ceremony in Riverfront Stadium in Cincinnati honoring him for his work in the field of drug addiction, he said he wished he could look down to third base and see a black manager on the coaching line.

At fifty-three, when death came after a second heart attack on October 23, 1972, in his Stamford, Connecticut, home, Robinson had become a national legend. His funeral in Manhattan was attended by local, state, and national figures. He was buried in Brooklyn, a few miles from the site of old Ebbets Field—where it all began.

Joy in Philly:
Robin Roberts

It was the final day of the 1950 season and Ebbets Field, the home of the Brooklyn Dodgers, was in an uproar—for a pennant was in the balance. The Dodgers trailed the Philadelphia Phillies by one game. A victory for the home-town club would mean a play-off for the league championship.

The game turned into a bitter hurling duel. Don Newcombe pitched for Brooklyn. On the mound for the Phillies was a stout-hearted, strong-armed youngster who was making his third start in five days in a valiant effort to bring a flag to Philadelphia. Despite fatigue and little or no batting support from his teammates, he kept blazing his fast ball past the tough Brooklyn hitters, and the Phils were leading 1–0 going into the last of the sixth. Then came a break which might have discouraged a lesser pitcher. Peewee Reese, of the Dodgers, drove the ball up against the scoreboard with two out. It looked like a legitimate double. But then something happened—or rather it didn't happen. The ball failed to come down. It stuck between the scoreboard and the right-field wall, and Reese raced all the way around the bases for a home run, tying the score. It was a freak home run, but it counted just as much as a blast into the seats.

Robin Roberts shook his head grimly and went back to work. Disaster threatened again in the last half of the ninth. Cal Abrams drew a pass and galloped to second on Reese's single. When Duke Snider followed with a one-base hit to center, Abrams headed for the plate with the winning run. Brooklyn fans jumped to their feet as Richie Ashburn in center field raced in, grabbed the ball with one hand, and fired toward the plate. Ashburn wasn't noted for having a particularly strong arm, but now he got off the greatest throw of his career. It was a "strike": Abrams was out by a whisker. Roberts, however, was still deep in hot water, for he had Reese on third and Snider on first with only one out. A fly ball could still win the game for the Dodgers and tie up the pennant race.

JOY IN PHILLY

Roberts gave dangerous Jackie Robinson an intentional pass to fill the bases and set up a force play at any base, particularly home. Carl Furillo, always a rugged hitter, came to the plate. Roberts worked coolly and carefully. He made Furillo foul out, and then he got Gil Hodges on a fly to right. The Dodgers had failed to score. It was one of the most exciting half innings in baseball history, and a great exhibition of grit and courage by a truly fine pitcher.

After that close call the Phillies put the pennant on ice. The first two men singled in the tenth inning. There was a force play, and then Dick Sisler, son of the famed first baseman George Sisler, hit into the stands for a home run. His big sock won the pennant and put the Phils in the World Series for the first time since 1915. And Robin Roberts became the first Philly 20-game winner since Grover Cleveland Alexander in 1917.

Speed, control, and stamina were a few of the qualities that made Roberts a great pitcher. Those, and coolness under fire. In fact he recalls being nervous only once. That was when he pitched his first major-league game. He was only twenty-one and had had only two months' experience in professional ball with Wilmington, when he was thrown into a night game against the Pittsburgh Pirates at Shibe Park. He walked the first man, Stan Rojeck. Then he struck out the second man and the nervousness disappeared. He lost, however, to Elmer Riddle, 2–0; but he had pitched a highly commendable game.

Robin, a big (six feet one and a half inches, 190 pounds), good-looking, dark-haired boy, was the workhorse of the Philly staff from 1950 on, pitching more than 300 innings each year. He frequently volunteered to work with only two days' rest, and once pitched three complete games in seven days and won all three. He won 28 games in 1952, highest total for a National League pitcher since Dizzy Dean in 1935.

He had a very smooth motion and didn't appear to be working too hard, which was undoubtedly one reason for his durability. His best pitch was his fast ball. "I just try to move it around on all of them," he said. "That is, high and inside and then low and outside, and so on. Naturally, if I know a batter has a particular weakness, I'll try to work on it. Trouble is, in the majors most any batter is likely to hit any pitch any time."

Watching Roberts out on the mound, you got the impression that he was angry at the batter. He appeared to seethe inwardly at times and to regard the hitter as a personal enemy. He faced the batters with barely repressed resentment and anger—as if their very presence were an insult. Even his teammates were sometimes surprised at the inward storm of the man. But it was one of the things that made him a great competitor.

Roberts was the type of pitcher who was seldom relieved even when he was trailing. Philly managers generally figured that if Robin couldn't stop the opposition nobody could. He once pitched 28 straight complete games.

Philadelphia's pride and joy was born in Springfield, Illinois, September 26, 1926, and was christened Robin Evan Roberts. He was the fifth of six children born to Thomas and Sarah Roberts. His father came from Wales and his mother from England. Married abroad, they immigrated to the United States in 1921.

Robin went to school in Springfield, attending Lanphier High. He was an above-average student, even though he preferred athletics to books and went from one sport to another as the seasons changed. He was good at baseball and football, but he gained early recognition as a high-scoring forward on the basketball team.

As an Air Corps trainee in 1944, he played against Michigan State, and made such an impression on the university coaching staff that when he was discharged from the Air Corps a year later he was given a basketball scholarship. He starred for the Spartans for three years.

The following spring, when he went out for the baseball team, he thought of himself as an outfielder or third baseman. "I wasn't hitting very well though," he explained, "and I wasn't running too well either. So I thought I'd try pitching."

It didn't look as though he'd make it at first. He went against Western Michigan College and was battered for a 9–1 loss. His second start was something different, however. Taking the mound against Great Lakes, he came through with a brilliant no-hitter, winning the game 8–0.

Robin learned a good bit about pitching from State's coach, John Kobs, and he learned some more in a college-manned resort league in Vermont in the summer. It was there in 1947 that a Philadelphia scout, Chuck Ward, spotted him and thought there might be something good for the Phillies. Ward chased him halfway across the country, caught up with him in Chicago, and signed him to a contract with a $25,000 bonus. That bonus, incidentally, meant a new home for his parents in Springfield.

Roberts moved back to Michigan State, insured his degree in physical education, and then reported to the Phillies' spring-training camp. He showed moderately well in the camp and was sent to Wilmington, a Class B minor-league team. Roberts stayed two months with Wilmington. He appeared in eleven games, won nine, and lost one, averaging eleven strike-outs a game.

Meanwhile the Phillies were running into trouble. They needed another starting pitcher desperately, so they decided to bring up young Robin Roberts and give him a chance. They never regretted that decision.

Called in about midseason, the young right-hander won seven games and lost nine for the sixth-place Phils. He was still pretty green, and he had to learn about major-league pitching simply by doing it. The following year, 1949, he worked 227 innings while winning fifteen games and losing the same number.

The Philly management was now in the process of building a pennant winner. They finished third in '49, but Roberts, Curt Simmons, Del Ennis, Granny Hamner, Richie Ashburn, Willie Jones, and others were beginning to get the hang of things in the big leagues. They were called the "Whiz Kids," and they furnished the climax to a long rebuilding program and youth movement launched by owner Bob Carpenter shortly after he took over the perennially second-division outfit in 1943. Average age of the regular line-up was twenty-six, while the club's top seven hurlers averaged a little over twenty-seven. A veteran relief pitcher, Jim Konstanty, was added, and he proved invaluable. He made many trips from the bull pen in moments of crisis and saved many games for the Phils.

It was a strange race in 1950. The Phillies looked like easy winners. On Labor Day, leading the league by seven games, they faced the Giants in a doubleheader at Shibe Park (later named Connie Mack Stadium). The New Yorkers had a pair of rough pitchers in Jim Hearn and Sal Maglie, and they dropped manager Eddie Sawyer's team twice. A couple of nights later in a twi-night double bill, Don Newcombe, ace of the Dodgers, almost pulled an iron-man stunt on the Phils. He held them to three hits and beat them 2–0 in the first game. Then he came back and hurled the first seven innings of the second game. He was taken out for a pinch hitter, with the Phils leading 2–0. The Dodgers, held to one hit in eight innings, woke up in the ninth, scored three times, and won the game 3–2. The next night Brooklyn won again, by the same score.

The Phillies were in trouble now. They weren't hitting, and their left-handed ace, Curt Simmons, had been called by the Army—and the Brooklyn club was winning steadily. The big lead was disappearing like snow in the springtime.

On September 29 the standings showed the Phils only two games in front of the Dodgers and scheduled for a pair at Ebbets Field. They had only to win one of the games to clinch the pennant. Should they lose both, the season would end in a deadlock. On the last day of September the Dodgers won, behind Erv Palica, 7–3, and that set the stage for the big October 1 finale—and Robin Roberts' twentieth victory. It had been a close call, but the Phillies had finally made it.

Philadelphia was wild with joy after the 4–1 ten-inning clincher at Brooklyn, and the citizens couldn't do enough for the club. After all, it was the first Philadelphia pennant since the Athletics' American League triumph in 1931.

The World Series was another story. It was strictly for the pitchers, and the Yankees were strong and rested. On opening day Jim Konstanty pitched brilliantly for Philadelphia, but Vic Raschi was better. He held the Whiz Kids to two hits, retired them in order in seven of the nine innings, and won the game 1–0.

The hard-working Roberts went to the mound the second day, and he too pitched wonderfully well. He and Allie Reynolds of New York quickly tied up in a fine duel. The Yanks got the jump in the second inning. With two out, Roberts walked Joe Coleman. The next hitter was Reynolds, and he was never much of a threat at the plate. But this time he swung late and got himself a single to right field. Running with two out, Coleman made it to third, and scored the first run of the game when Gene Woodling got an infield hit. It wasn't much of a show of power, but the Yanks had a run.

The Phils fought back and tied it up in the fifth on a pair of singles and Ashburn's scoring fly. Roberts and Reynolds dueled for the next four innings, and the Phils almost won it for Robin in the last half of the ninth when Hamner doubled with one out. A pinch hitter was passed, and the next batter, Mike Goliat, made the Yankee strategy look good when he bounced into a double play. Lightning struck in the top of the tenth inning when Joe DiMaggio, still a great ball player, hit into the left-field stands for a home run. It won the game; it beat Roberts; and it just about wound up the Series, although there were still two games to go.

The Whiz Kids battled hard for the third game, but lost it in the last half of the ninth inning.

The next day saw the end of the Series and a clean sweep for the New Yorkers, who won the game 5–2. Roberts came back in relief and got the Yanks out in the eighth inning of the losing cause. The Phils were not disgraced. Every game, with the possible exception of the last one, had been fiercely contested, and had the breaks gone the other way the Phils might have taken two or even three.

The game, hard-fighting team that had grabbed the National League pennant in 1950 and snarled defiance at the Yankees in the World Series fell to pieces in 1951. At no time did it threaten the leaders as it wound up in fifth place. The attack, not too powerful at best, suffered from injuries to Del Ennis, Dick Sisler, and Andy Seminick. These were the men the Phillies counted on for the long ball, and when they slumped or were out of the line-up there were few runs for the pitchers to work with. Richie Ashburn tried to carry the load himself. He had a good year; he hit .344 and finished second to Stan Musial. But Richie was not a long-ball hitter.

Curt Simmons was still in the Army, and Konstanty, the heroic "fireman" of the previous year, fell off badly, winning only four games. The powerful Roberts, however, continued his great work on the mound, rolling up 21 victories.

Robin was the sensation of baseball in 1952. With a fourth-place club (the Phils trailed the Dodgers, Giants, and Cards), he racked up the astounding total of 28 wins against only 7 defeats. He pitched 330

JOY IN PHILLY 189

innings and 30 complete games. And he walked only 45 men all season. In 9 of his complete games he did not issue a walk, and in 11 others he walked but one. His exceptional control gave him an average of only 1.36 walks per nine innings.

One of the most remarkable games of his career came on September 6 at Shibe Park. It was the first game of a twi-night double bill with the Boston Braves, and Roberts "didn't have it." That is to say, he was not at his best by any means. Yet look what happened.

When the Phillies came to bat in the last half of the eighth inning, they were trailing the Braves 6–2. But at this point they solved Boston rookie Virgil Jester for four runs and tied the score. Now back in the ball game, Roberts went to work.

He had it cut out for him. Hit for nine wallops previously, he was in trouble constantly. It wasn't one of those nice days when he had all his "stuff" and easily took care of the toughest batters. The fine edge of his control was gone, and he was either missing the strike zone or coming in right over the plate with a pitch that was too good. Yet he stayed in there and fought back.

With two out in the top of the ninth, Johnny Logan singled and Earl Torgeson whaled a long drive to right. Logan, trying to score, was trapped between third and home and tagged out. In the tenth Sid Gordon started with a single, but Roberts held fast. In the twelfth Torgeson and Gordon led off with singles. The next batter was the Braves' sensational rookie third baseman, Eddie Mathews, who had already hit a triple and a home run. It looked like the finish for Roberts, as though the Braves were finally ready for the kill. But Robin grimly fired away and forced Mathews to hit back to him. Roberts' throw forced Torgeson at third. Then came a rugged pinch hitter, Walker Cooper. Roberts was still in trouble; but he made Cooper hit on the ground, too, and the result was an inning-ending double play.

In the fourteenth inning, Logan led off with a single; in the fifteenth, Jack Daniels led off with a double. And so it went, with Roberts always in a jam but somehow managing to hold off the run that would mean the ball game. The seventeenth inning marked the first in the past ten in which Boston hadn't put a man on base. Meanwhile relief pitchers Sheldon Jones and Bob Chipman had blanked the Phils for eight innings, allowing only three hits.

The end came suddenly in the last half of the seventeenth. The first man up was Del Ennis, and he clubbed a home run into the left-field seats. Roberts had his twenty-third victory of the season—but only after three hours and fifty minutes of the toughest kind of work.

Watching this game was John (Hans) Lobert, a great third baseman of an earlier era. As the Phillies tied the score in the eighth inning, he turned to a friend and said: "That Roberts has a bulldog spirit. Nobody is going to beat him. He's as great as Alex

[Grover Cleveland Alexander] and Matty [Christy Mathewson] ever were." This was high praise indeed.

In this, his big season, Roberts didn't exactly get off to a running start. By mid-June his record was an unexciting 7 and 5. But from that time on he was practically invincible. His whirlwind pace over the last three and a half months of the season found him the winner in 21 out of 23 decisions.

The Phillies were back in the scramble for the National League pennant in 1953. They got off fast, winning 10 of their first 12. Then they slipped somewhat. Even so, it was an exciting race for a part of the season between the Dodgers, Milwaukee Braves, St. Louis Cardinals, and the Phils. In the final analysis the Brooklyn entry had too much power to be denied the pennant.

The hard-working Roberts broke his own record by pitching 347 innings. The durable ace was almost never taken out of a game, and bull-pen pitchers rarely bothered to warm up when he was on the mound. Starting August 24, 1952, he pitched 28 complete games in a row. The end of the streak came in Philadelphia July 9, 1953. He was leading the Dodgers 4–3 in the top of the eighth when the Brooklyn team belted him for two runs, including a triple by Gil Hodges. That did it. Roberts was kayoed for the first time in almost a year. Bob Miller came on the scene with some fine clutch pitching and held Hodges at third. In the Phils' half of the same inning, pinch hitter Smokey Burgess slammed a double, driving in two runs. Konstanty stopped the Dodgers in the ninth and the Phils had the game, 6–5, despite Roberts' knockout.

Robin didn't brood about the end of his streak. Three days later he started another one by beating the Pittsburgh Pirates 6–4.

Toward the end of the season, as Brooklyn pulled away from the rest of the league, main interest centered in the fight for second and third places. Milwaukee's Braves grabbed second; the Phils and Cards battled hotly for third and finally wound up in a tie.

It looked for a while as though Robin would win 30 games in 1953, but the strain of pitching so often was apparently too much even for the rugged Michigan State alumnus. "I wasn't conscious of being tired," he said, "but I must have been because I sure had trouble getting those fellows out, especially [Solly] Hemus and [Roy] Campanella!"

It still added up to a good season for the Philadelphia star. He won 23 games, the fourth straight year in which he was over the 20 mark. He was in a nice high income bracket by this time, too, with an estimated $40,000 a year.

His off-season activities included a weekly television show aimed at youngsters in the Philadelphia area, and personal appearances for the club. He was idolized by his young fans, who waited for him outside the television studio and, of course, outside the ball park after a game.

Roberts continued to deliver his own special brand of high-grade pitching for the Phillies until 1962, when he was traded to Baltimore in the American League. He was sent on to Houston in 1965 and closed out his great career there in 1966.

A strong, rugged pitcher with speed, control, and a fighting heart, Robin Roberts was one of the best right-handed pitchers that ever came down the pike.

Yankee Siege Gun: Mickey Mantle

In the middle of the 1958 season the New York Yankees were involved in a tense struggle in the nation's capital. It was the last half of the ninth inning, and the Washington Senators, trailing the American League champions 6–5, were putting on a last-ditch rally. They had men on second and third with two out. The batter lined a vicious drive toward right center, and the capital crowd jumped to its feet with a roar. Two runs would score—the Senators would win!

But streaking across the green outfield grass came

the fastest man in baseball. It was always a thrill to watch Mickey Mantle run. Going down to first base sometimes he was just a blur. Now in this ninth-inning crisis he turned on everything he had. Cutting diagonally toward the right center-field wall, he threw up his glove at the last second. It was unbelievable—but he had caught the ball for the third out. The disconsolate Washington fans filed out of Griffith Stadium, muttering to themselves.

It was a wonderful catch, but actually Mickey Mantle wasn't noted for his great fielding. He followed the incomparable Joe DiMaggio in the center-field spot for the Yankees when he was only nineteen years old, and he wasn't the superfielder that DiMaggio was. But his determination and his terrific speed made him a better than competent "gardener." At the bat Mickey was something special. He was a switch hitter (batted left-handed against right-hand pitchers and right against lefties)—and just about the best one that ever came into baseball. Batting from either side of the plate, he hit some of the longest home runs ever seen. He almost hit one all the way out of Yankee Stadium. It's never been done—but Mickey's shot landed in the last row of the right-field bleachers. Another time he hit over the monuments in center field.

A three-time winner of the Most Valuable Player award, Mantle hit 536 homers in his career and appeared in 2,401 games for New York, the most in Yankee history. Mickey played in 65 World Series games and 16 All-Star encounters. His 18 Series home runs are tops in that department. In 1956 he won the Triple Crown, with the highest batting average, the most runs batted in, and the most homers. And in 1961 he clouted 54 homers as he carried on a fantastic season-long four-base duel with teammate Roger Maris, who wound up hitting 61 to break Babe Ruth's long-standing record. He was some kind of ball player, that Mickey.

If he had a fault, it was striking out—and it infuriated him. He came to the bench on one occasion after fanning and kicked the water cooler viciously. Manager Casey Stengel looked up. "Ain't that water cooler that's striking you out," he said calmly.

But despite his strike-outs, Mickey's booming hits and speed on the base paths and in the outfield made him a solid star and a fixture with one of the most successful of all baseball organizations—the New York Yankees.

Much credit for Mickey's success must go to his father, E. C. ("Mutt") Mantle, a former baseball player himself who started grooming Mickey for the diamond almost before he could walk. Mickey was born October 20, 1931, at Spavinaw, Oklahoma, and Mutt Mantle, after a hurried conference with his wife, named the boy after the great catcher Mickey Cochrane. Mutt could hardly wait to get his boy into a uniform.

The youngster started becoming the world's greatest switch hitter at the age of five; here's how it happened. He was naturally right-handed, but his father decided that by starting young enough the boy could develop equal facility from either side of the plate. Mutt was right-handed, but Mickey's grandfather was a lefty. They took the boy into the back yard and, using tennis balls, took turns pitching to him. When his father was throwing, Mickey had to bat left-handed; and when his lefty grandfather was tossing the tennis balls, the youngster hit from the right side. It wasn't easy and the little boy complained bitterly, but one day he suddenly realized he could hit as well from one side as the other. That's how it started.

As he grew older he branched out into other sports. He was better than good at basketball and football as well as baseball. His basketball coach in junior high school at Commerce, Oklahoma, Frank Bruce, smiled as he recalled Mickey at the age of eleven.

"I had fourteen boys on the squad," he said, "and I mentioned something about needing one more. Somebody suggested Mickey Mantle, so I called him in.

"He weighed only 82 pounds and was three feet ten. He had two outstanding upper front teeth, big freckles all over his arms, face, and neck. And exceptionally long arms, which, with his sloping shoulders, made him walk something like a gorilla.

"I asked him why he hadn't come out for the team before. He looked up with a shy smile. 'Didn't think I could make it,' he said simply."

He may have been a shy kid, but his speed was phenomenal. He was the smallest boy on the squad, but he was the fastest. And he became the key player on a team that ran up an incredible three-year record.

Mickey, his coach noted, had a fiercely competitive spirit, and it was this that made the difference. "He was seldom the top scorer," Bruce pointed out, "but invariably it was his points that pulled out the close games." Led by young Mantle's speed and fight, Commerce won 120 games and lost just 6 in three years.

Mickey was a good football player, too, and he starred in the Commerce backfield. But it was here that his athletic career almost came to a sudden stop. During a pile-up at the line of scrimmage he was kicked in the left shin. Of course it hurt, but Mickey rubbed it and stayed in the game.

Unaccountably the pain continued, and finally an Oklahoma City specialist diagnosed the trouble: osteomyelitis. This is a bone disease—one that can't be checked easily.

For Mickey—and his father—it seemed like the end of the world. The boy was actually on crutches for a period and his athletic career appeared doomed. But thanks to sulfa drugs and diathermy, he was able to throw away the crutches after a few months. Nevertheless he had to have regular treatments down through the years to keep the disease under control, and that was the reason he was rejected for service with the Armed Forces.

In addition to his school team, Mickey also played in the Ban Johnson League for amateurs. Here he was spotted by Tom Greenwade, a Yankee scout. Greenwade watched the sixteen-year-old youngster, hitting from both sides of the plate, rap out a single, double, and homer. Then he got together with Mickey and his father and signed the boy to a Yankee contract—with a $1,100 bonus.

That was what father and son had been working for through the years: a big-league chance. The bonus wasn't great, but to be tied up with the fabulous New York Yankees was a dream come true.

The "Oklahoma Comet" spent two years in the minors with Independence of the K-O-M League and Joplin in the Western Association. His speed and terrific hitting brought him to the Yankees in 1951 as one of the game's most heralded rookies.

Mantle stayed with the club through spring training, and was still on hand when it left for Washington to open the 1951 season. But he had no idea whether or not he would be in the starting line-up. On the train Stengel gave him the news—Mickey was the Yankee right fielder. The youngster went back to his berth and lay awake shaking all night. But he was saved for the moment. When the Yanks got to Washington they found it was raining steadily, and the game was called off. The team returned to New

York, and on the day of their next game, the sun shone on Yankee Stadium. A jittery Mickey Mantle moved into right field against the Boston Red Sox. The first of his many major-league hits came in the sixth inning—a sharp single to left that knocked in a New York run.

The first of his homers came off Randy Gumpert in Chicago on May 1, and it was a real wallop—450 feet into the right-field seats. He was batting left-handed.

But there were troubles. First of all his fielding was still on the erratic side. He'd make a sensational running catch on one drive and then get lost on the next one. Stengel took to relieving him in the late innings when the Yanks were leading by a run or two.

Worse than that, however, were the strike-outs. The youngster kept his batting average at a respectable .300, but he was fanning too often. There was a double-header in Boston that almost drove him out of his mind. He struck out three times in the first game and twice in the second. "I can't get near the ball," he moaned to Stengel. The Yankees lost both games.

Mickey recognized the disaster signals. A few days later he got the bad news. It was back to the minors—Kansas City, then in the American Association. Naturally the boy was disappointed, but after a few black days he pulled himself together, and by August he was hitting a gorgeous .361 for the K.C. Blues. In New York the Yankee front office was getting reports on the young man's progress, and late in the season they pulled Mickey Mantle back to the parent club.

The Yanks were playing in Cleveland at the time, and Mantle contributed a two-run homer as they beat an old nemesis, Mike Garcia. This time the boy was back to stay.

The New Yorkers edged out the Cleveland Indians for the 1951 pennant. Playing in his first World Series was a right fielder by the name of Mantle—and he was also batting in the lead-off spot. The Yanks were up against their rivals from across the Harlem River. The Giants, who had arrived in the Series via Bobby Thomson's incredible home run in the final play-off game, were raring to go. But the Yanks, operating with their usual efficiency, wrapped it up in six games.

In the second game Mickey was knocked out with another injury. The Giants' Willie Mays hit a long one to right center between Mickey and Joe DiMaggio. Joe gave Mickey the green light and circled to back him up. Mickey was racing for the ball when he felt something snap in his knee. He slipped to the ground. In a flash the great DiMaggio reached over his shoulder and grabbed the ball. With the next motion Joe signaled to the bench for help. Mickey was out for the rest of the Series with a torn ligament in his right leg.

The injury healed over the winter, and by springtime the Oklahoma Comet was back in action. The old strike-out problem was still on hand, however, and he fanned 111 times in 1952 to lead the league in that unhappy department. But if he wasn't particularly proud of this feat, it should be noted that he hit for a .311 average and belted 23 home runs as the Yanks raced to another pennant. His homers were coming at opportune moments, too. There was the day in Chicago when the New Yorkers were trailing the White Sox 7–6 going into the ninth. With the bases full and two out—only one out away from defeat—Mickey stepped to the plate and faced Chuck Stobbs, a really good pitcher. Mantle hit the third pitch into the right-field stands and won the game for the Yanks.

The World Series was a rugged encounter, this time with the Brooklyn Dodgers. In the climax game at Ebbets Field, Mickey homered in the sixth and singled in the seventh to sew up the victory for the New York team.

As Mickey continued to slug the ball through the next few years he became one of the most feared batters in the American League. His total bases on balls were climbing steadily. With first base open, pitchers would rather pass him than take a chance on one of his big blasts.

The 1953 World Series saw the young man emerge as both hero and goat as the Yanks beat the Dodgers in six games. Mickey struck out eight times, five of them in succession. On the other hand his two-run homer won the second game, and in the fifth game he became one of the few men in history to hit a home run with the bases full in a World Series.

In 1956 the kid from Oklahoma put on a serious drive against Babe Ruth's home-run record. Back in 1927 the Babe had slugged out 60 homers. Nobody had since been able to even tie that record, although Jimmy Foxx and Hank Greenberg had come awfully close with 58. Now Mantle went on a four-base rampage and the newspapers started keeping score: "Today Mantle hit his 32nd. On this date in 1927 Ruth had 31." So it went for most of the season. Mickey kept socking the ball right-handed and left-handed. He didn't break the Babe's record, but he did have a wonderful season. This was the year he won the Triple Crown, with 52 homers, a .335 batting average, and 130 runs batted in. *The Sporting News* named him Major League Player of the Year, and nobody argued with the choice.

The World Series of 1956 was a victory for the Yanks over the Dodgers, and it produced a once-in-a-lifetime pitching epic by the Yankees' Don Larsen. On October 8, Don pitched the first perfect game in World Series history. Twenty-seven Dodgers came to the plate, and not one of them reached first base. It was a tremendous effort, and when the last man was retired catcher Yogi Berra tore out to the mound and jumped into the pitcher's arms. The police had to escort Don off the field.

During the off-season Mickey lived quietly with his

wife, the former Merlyn Johnson, whom he married in December, 1951. His principal hobbies have always been hunting and golf.

When the Yankees were traveling, he roomed with his long-time buddy Billy Martin, a firebrand infielder who set a World Series record with twelve hits in the six-game 1953 classic. The Mantle-Martin combination was broken up in 1957 by the famous but unfortunate Copacabana episode. Mickey, Yogi Berra, Hank Bauer, and Martin were quietly celebrating Billy's birthday in the New York night club. All were accompanied by their wives, with the exception of Martin, who was not married. The players were heckled from another table, a mild disturbance resulted, and there were front-page stories over a large part of the country.

The staid Yankee organization wouldn't tolerate this sort of thing, and although it was pretty well established that the Yankee party was innocent, Martin was sent to Kansas City a short time later. Thereafter Mickey roomed by himself when the team was traveling.

The year 1957 also marked an end to Yankee domination, although Mickey had a great year. His roaring .365 batting average was second only to Ted Williams'. He socked 34 home runs and had a slugging percentage of .665. The Yankees won the pennant by a comfortable eight-game margin but were outfought by the Milwaukee Braves in a hair-raising seven-game World Series.

It was no fun at all for Mickey. His leg was bothering him toward the end of the season. The trouble was diagnosed this time as "shin splints." At any rate Mickey was very uncomfortable. He started the Series in center field, but it was soon apparent that he wasn't the Mickey of old. A shoulder injury, caused when a Brave infielder fell on him in an attempted pick-off play, also handicapped his throwing and batting. This injury apparently carried over to the 1958 season.

But Mickey had a good year in 1958. He banged the ball for a .308 average and led the American League with 42 home runs. In the World Series he hit two home runs and sparked the late Yankee charge that carried the New Yorkers to a thrilling victory over Milwaukee.

Mickey Mantle was still a fine ball player through the early '60's, but eventually the ailing legs which had caused him so much pain for so long brought an end to his magnificent career. In 1967 manager Ralph Houk shifted him to first base, where he wouldn't have to move around so much. But the following year, still at first, Mickey had his poorest season as a Yankee. He batted .237 with only 18 home runs. The handwriting was on the wall, and the following spring he announced his retirement.

"I can't play anymore," the thirty-seven-year-old Mantle told a packed news conference at the Yankees' spring-training hotel in Fort Lauderdale, Florida. "I don't hit the ball when I need to. I can't steal when I need to. I can't score from second when I need to." After eighteen years he had reached the end of the trail. It was all rather sad. Mickey was one of the greats.

Wings on His Feet: Willie Mays

During the 1950's, '60's, and early '70's when National League people got together and discussed the stars of their league, they seldom mentioned Willie Mays. They just said "Willie" and let it go at that. Everybody knew whom they meant.

He joined the New York Giants as a nervous twenty-one-year-old center fielder in 1951, and in the years to follow he became a National League legend —an all-time great, the finest all-round player of his era.

Willie Mays, in his prime, employed a combination

of skills that made him unique among ball players. He had a good batting eye, plus power, speed and intelligence on the bases, a strong throwing arm, and the ability to judge the direction and distance of a ball hit to the outfield. In fact, there was no skill belonging to an outfielder in which Willie was short of superlative.

There was the time the Giants were playing the Dodgers and the score was tied in a late inning. The Dodgers had Billy Cox, a fast man, leading off third with one out when Carl Furillo hit a deep fly to right center. Willie tore across the field, but he, a right-hander, was traveling in the wrong direction to make the throw that would get Cox at the plate. But look what he did. He grabbed the ball in his gloved hand, pivoted in a full circle on his left foot, and blazed the ball toward the plate.

The play was as close as your next breath, but Cox was out—and the Giants eventually won the game. Said one coach: "Willie will have to do that again before I believe it."

In a World Series game against Cleveland, Vic Wertz hit a terrifically long high drive to dead center field in the Polo Grounds. Willie turned his back on the plate and started sprinting. On the dead run he caught the ball as it came over his shoulder, 460 feet from home plate!

Many honors came his way. Willie was National League Rookie of the Year, Outstanding National League Player, and twice Most Valuable Player. He was a regular for the National League in the annual All-Star game. In the space of four years—some of that time spent in the Army—Willie sparked the New York Giants to two pennants and one world championship. Then, after the team moved to the West Coast, he led San Francisco to the 1962 National League pennant.

It all began in Fairfield, Alabama. A young steelworker named William Howard Mays and his wife, Ann, had a baby on May 6, 1931. It was a boy and they named him Willie—not William.

Willie's father was a semi-pro outfielder, so the boy learned to catch and throw almost before he could walk. He started playing with school teams—but not only baseball. Like so many major-league stars, Willie as a boy was good at almost all sports. However, his father concentrated on baseball with him, and when the boy was fourteen he was playing on the same team with his dad!

He was attending Fairfield Industrial School at the time, and despite all his athletic activities, he did remarkably well in class. In fact the principal and the athletic coach both urged him to go on to college.

Willie was only sixteen when his father got him a chance with the Birmingham Barons, a professional club. They took him on as a utility outfielder. This, of course, made him ineligible for any of the school teams. He kept up with his studies, however, and graduated with his class.

Then the regular center fielder for the Barons was

hurt, and Willie took over. When the regular recovered from his injury, his job was no longer open: Mays was there. With the Barons, as in later years with the Giants, Willie Mays was the life of the party. Happy, carefree, completely uninhibited, he kept the Barons relaxed whether they were in a tough game on the field or riding a bus to the next town.

He came to the attention of the New York Giants only by accident. The Giants' Sioux City club needed a first baseman badly and called on the parent organization. There was a man in the Negro National League who, it was thought, might possibly be able to help out, and scouts were dispatched to look him over.

What they saw was an accomplished player but a man too old for consideration. However, the scouts' trip was far from a total loss. They saw a center fielder for the Barons who appeared to be doing just about everything that could be expected of a ball player.

In a few days Willie Mays was Giant property—one of the best moves ever made in the club's long history. He was sent to Trenton, where he played 81 games and whacked Interstate League pitching for a .353 mark. The next year Willie was promoted to Minneapolis, of the American Association. He was terrific. He hit .477 in 35 games, and there were loose boards in the fence where Willie hit it with his ripping line drives.

Willie never drank or smoked. A teammate once

said the worst thing he ever did was take a bath. But Willie liked to go to the movies. He was sitting in a Minneapolis theater when an usher found him and told him he was wanted at the baseball office.

This was it: the Giants had decided to cut short his minor-league training and bring him up right away. It was 1951, remember, and the Giant management figured it had a good team. With a little help it could go all the way.

Willie was twenty-one years old—and he was scared. He joined the Giants in Philadelphia, where they were engaged in a series with the Phillies. Willie's heart was thumping as he trotted out to center field in the last half of the first inning. To his surprise nothing much happened. He handled himself adequately, but he failed to hit. He was blanked in the second game, too, and actually didn't get his first hit until the team returned to New York. At the Polo Grounds Willie socked one over the left-field roof— his first hit in the major leagues.

This was a good Giant team that Willie joined. Eddie Stanky, Alvin Dark, Monte Irvin, Bobby Thomson, Don Mueller, and Whitey Lockman were real pros. And there were pitchers like Larry Jansen, Sal Maglie, Dave Koslo, and Jim Hearn. But, strangely, this team could win little more than it lost through most of the season. In fact, on August 12, with only a month and a half to go, the Giants trailed the Brooklyn Dodgers by 13 games.

But just about then began one of the greatest

stretch drives in all baseball history. The Giants won and won and won, and the baseball world looked on in astonishment. For three weeks they could do no wrong—they won 16 games in a row.

The youngster from Alabama played a heroic role with his timely hitting and beautiful fielding. He was a real menace on the base paths, too. One writer said he ran the bases like a trail of lighted gunpowder.

Down through the remaining weeks of the season the Dodgers battled the Giants with everything they had. The Brooklyn team did not collapse; it played .500 ball, but the Giants kept gaining. They won 34 out of 41 games in this tremendous drive. On September 25 they beat the Phillies—and the Dodgers lost a double-header in Boston.

One game behind, two days to go. The Giants won and the Dodgers lost. All tied. The Giants won again, but Brooklyn fought back and in a long tough game with Philadelphia came out on top. The season ended in a deadlock.

The great city of New York practically lost its mind as the three-game series for the National League championship opened in Brooklyn's Ebbets Field. Naturally a more than capacity crowd was on hand, and it saw Monte Irvin and Bobby Thomson clout home runs to give the Giants the victory behind Jim Hearn's steady pitching.

Now the Dodgers were snarling. They had thought they had the pennant won in August. Today they were one game away from losing everything. They reacted violently and slammed the Giants all over the Polo Grounds to win, 10–0.

That brought it down to just one ball game; and as the Giants came to bat in the last half of the ninth inning, the Dodgers were leading 4–1. Alvin Dark and Don Mueller opened with a pair of singles. Monte Irvin was out on a short fly, but Whitey Lockman kept the Giants' rally alive with a double that scored one run and made it 4–2. There were runners at second and third when Bobby Thomson stepped to the plate. He took one strike and then hit the next pitch into the left-field stands to score three runs and win for the Giants 5–4. Young Willie Mays was in the "on deck" circle on one knee to watch that historic hit, which brought a pennant to the Polo Grounds.

The World Series was another story. The Giants were opposed by a tough, well-rested Yankee club, which stopped the Giant attack, held Willie Mays to four singles, and won the world title, four games to two.

That 1951 Series, however, was not without its thrills. In the third game Eddie Stanky pulled a daring stunt, later referred to as "the dropkick." The Giants were leading 1–0 in the fifth inning when Stanky drew a base on balls. The hit-and-run sign was on, and Stanky took off for second on the next pitch. But Yankee catcher Yogi Berra had anticipated such a move. He called for a pitch-out and threw straight down to Phil Rizzuto, covering second. Phil was waiting with the ball when Stanky slid in, but Eddie managed to kick the ball out of Rizzuto's hand and it rolled into short center field. Stanky promptly picked himself up and raced for third. There were some complaints about this maneuver, and actually we're not recommending it. Certainly nobody ever did it again to Rizzuto!

After that game the Yankees took charge of the Series. But it had been a fine year for the Giants' rookie center fielder. During the season Mays hit a respectable .274 and socked 20 homers. Although veteran Yankee pitchers held him in check during the Series, there was no doubt in anybody's mind that the boy from Alabama was in the big leagues to stay.

There was only one hitch—Willie was slated for Army service; and after he had played 34 games of the 1952 season the call came through.

With Mays gone most of '52 and all of '53, the Giants sank out of pennant contention. Of course, no one player carries a whole club, but it did seem as though the Giants were lost without Willie.

Two important things happened to the Giants in 1954. First of all, Willie Mays came back from the Army; and secondly, the club acquired Johnny Antonelli, a fine southpaw pitcher, from the Braves. Willie was overjoyed to be back in baseball, and the Giants as a team welcomed him with open arms. He showed his appreciation by leading the league with a .345 batting average. He was the same old Willie—a little older, a little stronger—and he hit a home run off Carl Erskine, of the Dodgers, in his first game back. Altogether he hit 41 that year, 6 in one five-game period. Antonelli showed his appreciation by winning 21 games and losing only 7.

He and Willie were a fine combination—too much for the rest of the league—and the Giants won the pennant with something to spare. In the World Series they met a Cleveland Indian team that had won 111 games, demoralizing the Yankees and the rest of the American League. The Indians were heavy favorites to trim the New Yorkers. But something happened.

The Giants, to the utter amazement of the whole baseball world, clobbered the Indians in four straight games to give the National League its first championship in eight years. Mays and Antonelli performed up to their billing; but it was a virtually unknown pinch hitter who came off the bench to wreck the American Leaguers. Dusty Rhodes hit two home runs and two singles in vital spots and knocked in seven big runs.

Mays kept rolling along, playing the game he loved and playing it very well. He once said he loved baseball so much he'd play for nothing. He never had to go that far, however, and he later became one of the higher-priced National League players. And he was worth every cent the Giants ever paid him.

For Willie 1955 was another banner year. He batted a solid .319 and clubbed out the imposing total of 51 home runs. On top of that he stole 24 bases. The team, however, finished in third place. Injuries plus a bad year for Antonelli ruined the Champions' chances of repeating. Even worse days were coming; for in the next two seasons—'56 and '57—the proud New Yorkers fell into the second division.

Mays kept up his scorching pace through 1957. He hit .333 and was second only to the St. Louis Cardinals' Stan Musial. Willie hit 35 home runs and 20 triples, which gave him a league-leading slugging percentage of .626. And he was still running wild on the bases. Thirty-eight times he took off for the next base and got away with it. Pitchers and catchers were getting very nervous when Willie was loose on the base paths.

Mays still had great years ahead of him when, in 1958, the Giants moved to San Francisco. In 1962 he hit .304 and crashed 49 homers as the Giants won the National League pennant after a tingling play-off series with the Los Angeles Dodgers. Willie's single in the ninth inning of the third game sparked a winning charge that carried his team into the World Series against the New York Yankees. The Series went the limit—down to the last half of the ninth inning of the last game when, for one shattering instant, either the Yankees or the Giants could have been World Champions.

With the Yankees leading 1–0, the Giants' Matty Alou was safe on a bunt single, and with two out Willie Mays came to the plate. The big San Francisco crowd screamed as Willie lined a double to left. Alou held third, and the dangerous Willie McCovey stepped in. A single would score two runs and win it all for the Giants. McCovey hit the ball like a bullet—but right at Yank second baseman Bobby Richardson. Bobby held the ball, and it was all over.

Mays continued his superior all-round play for the Giants, blasting 38 homers in 1963 and 47 in '64. He was named the league's Most Valuable Player again in 1965 after a sensational year in which he batted .317 and clubbed 52 homers. He cracked 37 homers the next year, and had another fine season in 1970, when he batted .291 with 28 homers.

But he was beginning to slow down a bit. It was inevitable. He had been racing around the bases and across the outfields of the big leagues since 1951. Now the end of a season found him exhausted. On May 11, 1972, Willie headed back for New York, where all the excitement had started. The Giants had traded him to the New York Mets.

The 1973 season must have convinced Willie it was time to say goodbye. He was forty-two years old; he was hitting only .211, he had lost much of his speed, his arm appeared to be gone. So he called a press conference at New York's Shea Stadium on September 20 and announced that he would retire at the end of the 1973 campaign. His future was assured. The Met owners had guaranteed him a spot with the organization for the next ten years at an annual salary of $50,000.

Mays had been sidelined with two cracked ribs as his Met teammates put on their incredible drive for the championship of the Eastern Division of the

National League. But he was on hand for the play-off series with the Cincinnati Reds, winners in the West. Willie's single in the fifth inning of the deciding game ignited a four-run New York rally that carried the Mets to a 7–2 victory and the National League championship.

Willie saw limited action in the first three games of the World Series, in which the Oakland Athletics edged the Mets four games to three for their second straight world championship. Mays contributed two hits and knocked in a run in the losing cause. It was his farewell to the game.

But he hated to leave. "It's hard to explain how much I love baseball," he said. "We've been going together for twenty-two years. It's a love affair."

In Quest of the Magic Number: Hank Aaron

The baseball spotlight glared down on the city of Atlanta, Georgia, as the 1973 season got under way. One of the sport's all-time-great hitters was nearing the close of his career and at the same time closing in on one of the game's most revered statistics. The Braves' right fielder, Henry Aaron, needed 41 home runs to tie Babe Ruth's career record of 714 four-base shots; and excitement mounted every time Henry banged one into the seats and moved one step closer to the Babe's mark.

"This is undoubtedly the most important record

we'll see broken in our time," said Paul Richards, the astute general manager of the Braves. The fans agreed with him.

In 1961 Roger Maris, of the New York Yankees, had broken Ruth's season record of 60 homers, and the pressure in the dying days of the season surely shortened the playing career of a truly fine outfielder. Now the sports world watched to see how "Hammerin' Hank" Aaron would react to the strain.

The pleasant and soft-spoken Aaron had arrived at this critical point in his baseball life by consistently hitting the long ball through nineteen big-league seasons. After 13 homers as a rookie in 1954, he never had fewer than 24 in any single year. He was thirty-nine years old as he reached out for the Ruthian crown. The Babe was forty that historic day in May, 1935, when, as a member of the Boston Braves, he rapped his 712th, 713th, and 714th homers at old Forbes Field in Pittsburgh.

Playing all his years for the same club (the franchise was transferred from Boston to Milwaukee and then, in 1966, from Milwaukee to Atlanta), Henry led the National League in homers on three occasions, and at the start of the 1973 season had crashed out 3,391 hits and compiled a career batting average of .311. He won the league's Most Valuable Player award in 1957 when he hit 44 homers, knocked in 132 runs, and batted .322. He hit .393 and .333 in two World Series and has been chosen for every National League All-Star team in the past eighteen years. No wonder pitchers call him "Bad Henry"—he has the "baddest" bat in baseball.

Henry Louis Aaron was born February 5, 1934, in Mobile, Alabama, the third of six children. His father, who was a construction worker, and his uncle and three brothers were all ball players. Young Henry couldn't have escaped from the game if he had wanted to—and he didn't want to. "If Henry wasn't at home, you knew he was over at the park playing ball," his mother said. "That's all he ever wanted to do." When he wasn't playing baseball, the youngster was reading about the sport, listening to it on radio, or watching it on television.

In his biography of Aaron, Joel M. Cohen reports that young Henry was so crazy about baseball his father once had to chase him out of a poolroom—not exactly a place where fathers like to find their young sons. Henry was supposed to be in school, but this was early October, 1951, and the New York Giants were meeting the Brooklyn Dodgers in the deciding game of a play-off series for the National League championship. Looking at the game on television, Henry followed every pitch, as the Giants finally won on Bobby Thomson's last-minute jackpot homer. Unluckily the boy's father, who was set on sending Henry to college, got off work a little early that day and decided to drop into the poolroom for a bit of relaxation. Both father and son were dismayed at the confrontation.

Henry attended Central High School and finished

at Josephine Allen Institute in Mobile. Neither school, however, had a baseball team, so Hank played softball during the spring and football during the fall. Incidentally, he turned out to be a first-class high-school halfback.

He started playing baseball seriously with the Mobile Black Bears, a semi-pro club, during his junior year at school, and at the end of the season was offered a contract by the barnstorming Indianapolis Clowns. The Clowns were part of the Negro American League, featuring some of the most talented black players in the country.

Hank eagerly accepted the offer from the Clowns and set off for Indianapolis carrying a battered suitcase, $2 in his pocket, and two sandwiches his mother had made for him. He was only eighteen when he broke in as a shortstop with the team. He wasn't great in the field, but he could certainly hit the ball. He was batting .467 when the Milwaukee Braves began to take an active interest in him. They signed him for $350 a month in 1952 and sent him to Eau Claire, Wisconsin, in the Northern League. He hit a neat .336 for the Class C team and was named the league's most outstanding rookie.

Next year Henry was promoted to the Jacksonville, Florida, Tars in the South Atlantic League. Jacksonville hadn't won a pennant in about fifty years. Then Henry, by now a second baseman, appeared on the scene. Hitting .362, with 22 home runs, Hank led the

Tars to the championship, and there was joy in Jacksonville.

Meanwhile the parent club, the Braves, found themselves loaded with infield talent and decided to convert Henry into an outfielder. He was sent to Puerto Rico to play winter ball and learn the new position. Although he did well, Henry was resigned to another year in the minors. Then Braves outfielder Bobby Thomson, obtained in a trade with the New York Giants, broke an ankle. The call went out for Aaron—and the twenty-year-old youngster was an outfielder for the Milwaukee Braves as the 1954 National League pennant race started.

Nervous at first, Hank soon began playing a kind of ball that made the fans forget the injured Thomson. He hit for a respectable .280 average, chipped in with 13 homers, and was runner-up to Wally Moon, of the St. Louis Cardinals, for Rookie of the Year honors.

There was no "sophomore jinx" operating for Henry Aaron. In his second year with the Braves he hit .314, with 27 homers. The following year he was good for 26 more circuit shots and upped his batting average to .328. The boy had become a six-foot, 180-pound man, and his big bat and strong, accurate arm were respected throughout the league. One day Jackie Robinson, Brooklyn's great star and Hank's early idol, was playing third, and refused to move toward the plate on a bunt situation with Aaron at bat. "Anytime you want to bunt, we'll give you first base," Jackie said later. "Just so you don't get anything more."

The Braves were in the process of putting together a really fine club. Seasoned hurlers Warren Spahn and Lew Burdette carried most of the pitching load, supported by a rugged cast that included Eddie Mathews, Wes Covington, Andy Pafko, Joe Adcock, and Bad Henry Aaron. By 1957 the Braves were ready to make a move for the pennant.

All season they fought a running battle with the St. Louis Cardinals; and on September 23 the two contenders clashed at Milwaukee with the Braves needing one game to clinch the league championship. In a tense struggle before a sellout crowd of 41,000, the rivals battled into the bottom of the eleventh inning with the score tied at 2–2. When Johnny Logan singled, the Braves had the pennant-winner on base. Two outs later he was still on base—and Hank Aaron came to the plate.

The home-town fans pleaded for a big hit, and they got it. Hank's forty-third home run of the season disappeared into the stands, and Milwaukee had the National League pennant.

It had been a great year for the young man from Mobile. He hit .322, knocked in 132 runs, and led the league with 44 homers. He easily won the Most Valuable Player award.

The Braves' opponents in the World Series were the always formidable New York Yankees. In a duel of southpaws, New York ace Whitey Ford edged Warren Spahn, 3–1, as the Series got under way in Yankee Stadium, with Aaron held to a single. Hank tripled and scored in the second inning as the Braves took the second game behind right-hander Lew Burdette and tied the Series. The Yankees reacted violently, and in the third game slammed the Braves 12–3 at Milwaukee. Two of the Milwaukee runs came on a homer by Hank.

Aaron's second Series homer came the next day when the Braves again tied the set with a 7–5 tenth-inning victory. The Braves took the lead for the first time when Lew Burdette came up with a brilliant 1–0 win in the last game at Milwaukee. Singles by Mathews, Aaron, and Adcock produced the only run of the game.

Now Milwaukee's hustling Braves were closing in on a world championship. They needed one victory in two games as the teams returned to Yankee Stadium. The champagne was ready to pop—but there was a slight delay while the Yanks' Bob Turley survived another Aaron home-run blast to beat the Braves, 3–2, and again tie up the Series.

But the Braves were not to be denied. They struck early in the deciding game and coasted home to the title, 5–0, behind another fine effort by the tireless Burdette. The Milwaukee Braves were Champions of the World.

Hank Aaron had had a great Series. He led both clubs with a .393 average, socked three homers and a triple, and had seven runs batted in. The Aaron family was proud and happy.

The Braves successfully defended their National League crown in 1958, getting serious opposition mainly from the Pittsburgh Pirates. The pennant clincher was a mid-September game at Cincinnati; Hank Aaron's thirtieth homer of the season was the difference in a 6–5 Milwaukee win. It was another fine year for Henry, who batted .326 and knocked in 95 runs.

The World Series was a rematch with the Yankees, and in the early going the Braves all but chased the New Yorkers out of the ball park. Behind Aaron's clutch hitting and the steady pitching of Spahn and Burdette, the Milwaukee entry took three of the first four games and was on the threshold of another world title. Then the roof fell in. The Yankees, rallying brilliantly, swept through three straight games, the last two in Milwaukee, to win the Series, four games to three. It was a heart-breaking loss for the Braves—but the Yanks hadn't been able to stop Aaron. Hank hit .333 with nine hits, including a pair of doubles.

Aaron continued to give Milwaukee fans the best kind of baseball; his .355 in 1959 was tops in both leagues. He was the complete ball player by this time. He hit with power to all sectors, fielded his position perfectly, used a strong and accurate arm to keep the base runners honest, and ran the bases himself with speed and intelligence.

On June 8, 1961, Hank, Eddie Mathews, Joe Adcock, and Frank Thomas became the first four players to hit home runs in succession in one inning. They did it in the seventh inning in a game against the Cincinnati Reds.

With all his success, Henry remained something of a loner. He was a serious professional, doing his job the way it should be done and doing it every day. For this he was well paid—he ultimately received a $200,000-a-year contract.

In 1966, the year the club moved to Atlanta, Hank gave his new fans something to cheer about when he led the league with 44 homers. His 39 the following year were enough to again take top honors. The 500th home run of his career came on July 14, 1968; it was hit off a good left-hander, Mike McCormick of the San Francisco Giants.

But more than home runs were piling up for Henry Aaron. The years were beginning to take their toll. He was thirty-seven, and the Brave management, thinking to preserve his legs and keep his potent bat around as long as possible, moved him to first base in 1971. Henry didn't like it much, and after two years he was back in the outfield. His once great throwing arm must have slipped a bit, too, because enemy base runners started moving from first to third on shots to right field. A few years back they wouldn't have been nearly so daring. So Henry moved to left field.

But he was as dangerous as ever at the plate. He hit 47 home runs in 1971, a career high, but this time not enough to lead the league. Pittsburgh's Willie Stargell picked that year to hit 48. Hank's 118 runs batted in moved him past Jimmy Foxx, Stan Musial, and Ty Cobb on the all-time major-league RBI list, into third spot behind Babe Ruth and Lou Gehrig.

Bad Henry hit the 600th homer of his career on April 27, 1971, in a 6–5 Atlanta loss to the Giants. The blow came off pitcher Gaylord Perry, who said earlier, "If he hits it off me he will have earned it." In 1972 Hank hit 34 more circuit blasts, and now everybody was talking about the assault on Babe Ruth's long-standing record.

On July 21, 1973, at Atlanta he hit No. 700. The blow came in the third inning on a fast ball from Philadelphia Phillies pitcher Ken Brett and threw the stadium into an uproar. The ball was retrieved in the left-field stands by an eighteen-year-old Atlanta youth, Robert Winborne, who received 700 silver dollars for the ball from the Brave management.

Now the pressure was on in earnest. Everywhere Hank went he was trailed by newspaper reporters, magazine writers, and, often as not, network television broadcasters. Fans hounded him for autographs, of course, and the mail—some of it abusive and racist, some of it encouraging—poured in. His phone was always ringing and he had trouble sleeping at night. Usually easy-going, Aaron lost his temper every now and then, snapped back at his tormentors. "Leave me alone. I'm just trying to do my job!" he barked on more than one occasion. Tension was

IN QUEST OF THE MAGIC NUMBER

mounting throughout the country to such a pitch that he had to have special police protection on entering and leaving a ball park.

Henry's fortieth home run of the year, and No. 713 of his career, came on the next to last day of the 1973 season. Now he had one more game in which to hit one more homer and tie the Babe. But it wasn't to be. He collected three hits as the Braves lost, 5–3, to the Houston Astros, but all three of the hits were singles. All they did was to bring his batting average for the season up to .301.

Babe Ruth's record was safe for another year—though just barely. Henry Aaron was on the rocky road to baseball immortality.

"Peace in Right Field": Roberto Clemente

Puerto Rico has sent many fine ball players to the major leagues, but none greater than the all-time favorite of Pittsburgh fans, the consistently brilliant Roberto Clemente. For eighteen years this superb athlete roamed the outfield with speed and sure-handed efficiency, and at the plate he supplied the ringing base hits that helped make the Pirates the power team of the National League.

Clemente was highly respected not only as a baseball player but as a man. His tragic death on New Year's Eve, 1972, saddened people the world over. Leading a mercy mission to earthquake-devastated Managua, Nicaragua, he was killed in a plane crash near San Juan shortly after take-off. Clemente died as he had lived. Maybe slugging Willie Stargell, his teammate, said it best: "Roberto was always trying to help someone."

Ranked as one of the game's great right fielders, the five-feet-eleven, 180-pound Buc star was National League batting champion four times, hitting a personal high of .357 in 1967. He had a career total of 3,000 hits—a level reached by only ten other players. He led the Pirates to two world championships, and in fourteen World Series games he connected for 21 hits and a .362 batting average.

Roberto played the outfield with utter abandon—some of the catches he made had to be seen to be believed. One day in Houston he was playing in right center when Bob Watson of the Astros, swinging late but hard, banged one down the right-field line. Clemente tore after the ball and hit the wall.

"He didn't run into that wall," said one observer. "He jumped into it!" Nevertheless he held on to the ball and saved the game.

Two days later in Pittsburgh's rain-soaked Three Rivers Stadium, Clemente raced after a fly ball, slid across the turf on his knees, and caught the ball with water spraying up all around him.

Roberto seemed to make this sort of catch all the time, and Pirate pitchers were delighted to have him out there. "Robby's playing today," right-hander

Steve Blass would say, "and there will be peace in right field." Pitchers felt that if a ball was hit to right and didn't leave the ball park, Clemente would somehow get to it. He almost always did.

Some writers claimed he had a stronger and more accurate arm than Willie Mays. At Forbes Field, the former Pirate ball park, Clemente once took a fly at the gate in deepest right field and threw on a line to the catcher. The distance: 460 feet.

Another day Willie Davis, fastest of the Los Angeles Dodgers, hit a blistering shot to right field and thought he had a sure double. Seeing the catlike Clemente getting quickly to the ball, Davis changed his mind and sped back to first—but too late. Roberto's throw went to first base like a bullet, and the unhappy Davis was tagged out.

Roberto Walker Clemente was born in Carolina, Puerto Rico, a small town near San Juan, on August 18, 1934. He was the youngest of seven children of Melchor Clemente, a sugar plantation foreman, and his wife, Luisa.

Early in life Roberto set his sights on a college education and a career as an engineer. But of course this plan would be scrapped as his love of baseball grew. At first he played softball in playgrounds and then in a municipal league. Later it was hardball on the sandlots. When he wasn't playing he was squeezing a hard rubber ball in his hand to strengthen the muscles in his throwing arm. That arm became one of the most powerful in the history of baseball. Once Clemente laughingly said he might have gotten his arm from his mother. When she was seventy-three years old, Luisa Clemente was asked to throw out the first ball at the opening game of a winter league in Puerto Rico. She didn't merely toss the ball out gently, as might have been expected. "She fired a hard strike from box seat to home plate," Roberto reported.

A natural athlete, young Clemente played baseball for his high-school team and starred on the track team, where he excelled at the high jump and javelin toss. While still in school, he played baseball for a semi-professional club in Santurce, Puerto Rico. One day he was spotted by a scout for the Brooklyn Dodgers. The Dodger organization offered to give him a $10,000 bonus if he signed with them, and Roberto accepted.

He was nineteen when he arrived in Montreal, home of the Dodger farm team in the International League. Actually he didn't get much of a chance with Montreal. The Dodgers had overextended themselves and simply had too many good outfielders in their organization. They let Clemente go to the Pittsburgh Pirates in November, 1954. Roberto joined the Pirates the following spring. He was little less than sensational for most of the next eighteen years.

The first of Clemente's 3,000 big-league hits came on April 17 against the Dodgers. It was a single to left off pitcher Johnny Podres, and a moment later he scored his first run on a three-base hit by Frank Thomas.

It wasn't until his second year, however, that Roberto really hit his stride. He pulled his batting average up to .311, and on July 25 he showed the speed and determination that were to mark his whole career. Arnold Hano tells the story in his biography of Clemente. Trailing the Chicago Cubs 8–5 in the last half of the ninth inning, the Pirates filled the bases with nobody out. Up came Clemente, and he swung on the first pitch. It was a vicious drive to deep left center, and the three Pirate runners raced home to tie the score.

Swinging around second and heading for third with throttle wide open came Roberto Clemente. Manager Bobby Bragan, coaching at third base, yelled and threw up both his hands to stop the runaway youngster, but Roberto, ignoring signs and shouted orders, swept on to the plate. It was close, but he was safe and the Pirates had the game, 9–8.

Bragan had wanted to hold Roberto at third because he figured that with nobody out it would be a relatively easy task to get him home with the winning run. But the rookie was running with just one thought in mind: to win the ball game then and there. Bragan shook his head—what could he say?

Clemente's brazen base running paid off for the Bucs on another occasion in a game with Cincinnati. He was on first and Bill Virdon on second when

Smokey Burgess banged a single to right field, where Wally Post, a gifted outfielder with a powerful arm, grabbed the ball and set himself to make a play. But there was no play to be made. The fast Virdon was nearly home and Clemente was racing to third. Post then did what many outfielders do: he tossed the ball in a slow, lazy arc to second to make sure Burgess didn't get an extra base. Looking over his shoulder, Clemente saw what Post was doing and never hesitated as he whirled around third in a headlong dash for the plate. He had scored from first on a single.

Roberto was something to watch as he rambled around the base paths. Turning first base, his arms pumping up and down, his head bobbing, he looked as though part of him were headed for the pitcher's mound and the other part to right field. Nevertheless he was a fast, intelligent base runner.

Clemente was one of the big guns as the Bucs stormed to a National League pennant in 1960. He hit .314, and was joined in the mighty Pittsburgh effort by men like Bill Mazeroski, Dick Groat, Don Hoak, Dick Stuart, and Bob Skinner. Vernon Law, Bob Friend, and Harvey Haddix, three fine starting pitchers, were backed up by top-drawer relief man ElRoy Face.

The World Series with the New York Yankees that year turned out to be one of the weirdest of all time. It started off quietly enough, with the Pirates winning the opener 6-4 at Pittsburgh. Then things started happening. The Yank batting order erupted, and the

New Yorkers crushed the Pirates in two straight games, 16–3 and 10–0.

The double shellacking, according to New York sportswriters, would surely destroy Pittsburgh's morale and permit the Yanks to wind up the Series in a hurry. But Clemente, Mazeroski & Co. had been coming back from defeat all season; a couple of beatings were not going to discourage them. Now they dumbfounded the experts by taking the next two games at New York, 3–2 and 5–2, and headed home for Pittsburgh leading in the Series three games to two.

Again the Yankees turned on their awesome power and all but wrecked the Buc pitching staff, winning the sixth game, 12–0. But again the Pirates bounced back. With Mazeroski's ninth-inning homer providing the coup de grace, Pittsburgh won the deciding game, 10–9. The Pirates were World Champions, and Roberto Clemente, hitting safely in each game, had come up with nine hits for a .310 average. The New Yorkers had scored an incredible 55 runs on 91 hits—and lost.

In 1961, as the Pirates battled unsuccessfully to defend their hard-won title, Roberto Clemente had one of his best years. He was batting king of the National League with a .351 average that included 23 home runs. Also, his hit in the tenth inning won the All-Star game for the National League, 5–4.

Through the next six years Clemente was at his peak, hitting well over .300 each season and playing the outfield as brilliantly as any man ever did. Close friends of the Pirate star felt he didn't get the public acclaim he deserved. They attributed it to the fact that Roberto didn't play in New York or Los Angeles, the big media centers, and so didn't get the full press treatment accorded men like Mickey Mantle, Joe DiMaggio, and Willie Mays.

His teammates appreciated the man on and off the field. Always ready with encouragement and help, Clemente had a profound impact on other players, particularly the youngsters. Manny Sanguillen, for instance, developed into a first-class ball player, but when he first came up from Panama to join the Pirates he was a confused young man. Clemente, who had faced similar problems as a rookie, helped the boy with the new language and with the unfamiliar big-league atmosphere and showed him how to deal with newspapermen.

Following the 1964 season, in which he led the National League with a .339 average, Clemente returned home to Puerto Rico, where he was introduced to a tall, beautiful girl named Vera Zabala. They were married November 24 and Roberto bought a home in Rio Piedras, not far from where his parents lived. The couple subsequently had three boys.

Clemente was batting king of the National League again in 1965 and 1967, reaching his high of .357 in the latter year. He wasn't a home-run hitter—29 in 1966 was his top figure—but his wicked line drives shot between the fielders and slammed against walls all over the league. He received the Most Valuable Player award in 1966, and the Pirate management showed its appreciation by signing him to a contract calling for $100,000 a year.

In 1970, a year in which Roberto Clemente hit a very solid .352, the Pirates fought their way into the pennant play-offs, but were beaten by the Cincinnati Reds in three straight games. The following year, the team led by Clemente, Sanguillen, Willie Stargell, Bob Robertson, and Richie Hebner stormed through the San Francisco Giants in the play-offs and marched into the World Series against a heavily favored, star-studded Baltimore Oriole club.

The Orioles lived up to their reputations as they won the first two games in Baltimore, 5–3 and 11–3. With only Clemente doing any consistent hitting (two doubles and two singles), the Bucs were in serious trouble when the Series scene shifted to Three Rivers Stadium in Pittsburgh. Finally the Pirates stopped the Orioles in the third game, 5–1. A missed signal set up the winning runs in the seventh inning. Clemente was safe on an error and Stargell had drawn a base on balls. Bob Robertson came to the plate and was ordered to lay down a sacrifice bunt in order to move the runners up a base into scoring position. The sign was flashed by the third-base coach, but Bob, who hadn't bunted all season, missed the signal. Not so Clemente—Roberto stood on second base waving his arms trying to call time. Play was not halted, however, and Robertson, swinging on the next pitch, knocked the ball over a 385-foot sign in right center for a three-run homer.

The Pirates, always a great comeback team, tied up the Series with a 4–3 win the next day, and then delighted their followers by taking the lead for the first time with a 4–0 victory behind Nelson Briles.

One defeat away from elimination, the Orioles snapped back with a nerve-wracking tenth-inning 3–2 win at Baltimore. Clemente's homer in the third inning was the only offensive gesture by the Pirates.

Baltimore's Mike Cuellar retired the first eleven Pirates in the deciding game, but Oriole nemesis Clemente broke the ice with a fourth-inning blast over the center-field wall. The Pirates scored the winning run in the eighth on a single by Stargell and a double by Jose Pagan. It was a fine 2–1 victory for Steve Blass, and it gave Pittsburgh the world championship. Roberto Clemente led all batters with a .414 average. He had played in fourteen World Series games and hit safely in every one.

In 1972, Clemente's last year, the great Puerto Rican hit .312 as the Pirates sailed to victory by eleven games in the National League's Eastern Division. Roberto's last regular-season base hit came on September 30, while the Bucs were beating the New York Mets, 5–0. It was No. 3,000, and he dedicated it to "the Pittsburgh fans and the people of Puerto Rico."

Meanwhile the Cincinnati Reds had taken charge

of the Western Division, winning by ten and a half games, so the old rivals clashed again in a fight for a World Series berth. Leading 3–2 in the last half of the ninth inning of the fifth and deciding game at Cincinnati, the Pirates appeared to have it won; but they blew the game. First up for the Reds was All-Star catcher Johnny Bench, and he instantly tied the score with a homer. Two singles and a wild pitch followed quickly, and the Reds—not the Pirates—were off to the Series.

The Bucs were a sad crew, but a worse disaster was coming up. When Managua, the capital of the Central American country of Nicaragua, was shattered by an earthquake, Roberto Clemente headed a committee to aid the victims. On December 31, the Pirate star and four other men left International Airport in San Juan in an old DC-7 cargo plane loaded with supplies for the people of Managua. Five minutes after taking off, the plane crashed into the Atlantic Ocean. An investigation by the National Transportation Safety Board later revealed that the aircraft was overloaded and had two bad engines.

Clemente's death was a national tragedy. People from all walks of life mourned the passing of this baseball player, for he was indeed a superstar—on and off the field.

The baseball world showed how it felt. The rule requiring a five-year waiting period after retirement was waived for Roberto, and the Pirate star was enshrined August 6, 1973, in the Baseball Hall of

Fame at Cooperstown, New York. Watching the ceremony were Clemente's eighty-four-year-old mother; his widow, Vera; and their three sons, Robertito, Luis, and Enrique.

"This is Roberto's last triumph," said Vera Clemente.

Carlton Conquers All: Steve Carlton

One of the outstanding pitching feats in the history of baseball was accomplished by a lean, towering, twenty-seven-year-old refugee from St. Louis, who had a salary fight with his boss—Gussie Busch, owner of the Cardinals—and wound up working miracles twice a week for a team that was among the worst in baseball. Steven Norman Carlton, instead of howling with rage when he was traded just before the start of the 1972 season from the St. Louis Cardinals, perennial pennant contenders, to the Philadelphia Phillies, perennial pushovers, gave his cap an extra tug, went out to the mound, and won 27 games for a team that finished dead last.

The baseball world was stunned. Nothing like it had ever happened before in the annals of the sport. The Phils were so bad they won only 59 of 156 games all season—and Steve pitched almost half of them. He lost 10 times, and in those 10 his team "supported" him with an offensive display that averaged only 1.6 runs per game.

For the year, Carlton led pitchers of both leagues not only in victories but also in complete games (30). He led the National League in innings pitched (346⅓), strike-outs (310), starting assignments (41), and earned-run average (1.98). During one shining period he joined pitchers Lefty Grove, Rube Marquard, and Carl Hubbell as the fourth left-hander in history to win 15 games in a row.

Carlton's 27 victories were the most ever won by a pitcher with a last-place club. The best previous effort was turned in by Frank Hahn, who won 22 and lost 19 for the cellar-dwelling Cincinnati Reds in 1901. Two pitchers earlier had won 27 games for second-division teams, and one of them did it twice. In 1922 Eddie Rommel, a fine knuckleball pitcher and later an American League umpire, won 27 and lost 13 for Connie Mack's seventh-place Philadelphia Athletics. Grover Cleveland Alexander was 27–15 with a sixth-place Phillies club in 1914 and 27–14 in 1920 with the Chicago Cubs, who tied for fifth place.

Philadelphia fans, showing their appreciation of the

Carlton magic, packed Veterans Stadium whenever Steve was slated to pitch, stayed away in large numbers when somebody else was scheduled. He was referred to as "the Franchise"—without him there would have been no team. In his first season with the Philadelphians, Steve established himself as the top gate attraction in the city's history, and the Phillies promptly made him the game's best-paid pitcher at $167,000 a year.

Carlton, a quiet, friendly type, took his astonishing success in stride. "Playing on a losing club is no guarantee you're going to lose," he said. "Each day is a new chance to win." And win he did.

"The team played good ball behind me," he added. "Whenever I pitched they seemed to feel they were in the game all the way." And they were. For Steve, the Phillies played better than they knew how—at least good enough to help him into eight shut-outs, nine one-run games, and five two-run games.

Steve was born in Miami, Florida, December 22, 1944, the only son of Joe Carlton, a maintenance man for an airline, and his wife, Anne. The couple also had two daughters. A large part of his boyhood was spent running barefoot through the Everglades chasing snakes and alligators. The strength and accuracy of his left arm were developed by throwing rocks. Steve claims he and his buddies were a fairly wild crew. "All that kept me from being a juvenile delinquent," he once said, "was the fact that I never got caught." It seems that the worst thing the boys actually did, however, was to break a few windows. When he entered high school Steve was a shy, skinny youngster. He was six feet three and weighed only 135 pounds. He was not a particularly good student and he didn't have much luck with the girls either. "It was hard for them to dig a skinny, crew-cut kid with braces," he said.

When he started throwing baseballs instead of rocks, the results compensated for other setbacks. In Little League, American Legion, and high-school play, he was all but unbeatable as a pitcher. Cardinal scout Chase Riddle spotted him in action, liked what he saw, and signed the gangling youngster to a St. Louis contract.

Under a special arrangement with the Cardinals, Steve was allowed to continue his education. He entered Miami-Dade Junior College, but he lasted only one semester. Later he told reporter John Flynn of the Philadelphia *Inquirer,* "I wasn't cut out for college, not then at least. I was a 'C' student in high school and very immature. . . . There was a great stress put on English and every time I had to get up and speak before a class I was so embarrassed and self conscious."

So Steve went to work for the Cardinal organization on a full-time basis. The first rung on the ladder was Rock Hill, of the West Carolina League, where he quickly flashed his strike-out ability by fanning 91 batters as he won 10 and lost 1, with an earned-run average of 1.03. That same year he was moved to

Winnipeg, of the Northern League, where he struck out 79 more batters in 12 games. He finished up 1964 with Tulsa, of the Texas League, and in 4 games disposed of 21 hitters by strike-outs.

Steve worked his way up to the Cardinals in 1965, appeared in 15 games, and then was sent back to Tulsa for further seasoning. Toward the close of the 1966 season he returned to the Cardinals; he stayed in St. Louis until he was sent to Philadelphia in the trade. In 1967, his first full year in the major leagues, he won 14 games and lost 9. When he added 13 more wins the following year, he appeared ready to step into a starring role with the usually potent St. Louis club.

Carlton slipped into a couple of World Series games those first two years in St. Louis. In 1967 he started the fifth game against the Boston Red Sox, gave up three hits and one run in six innings, but was charged with the 3-1 defeat after being removed for a pinch hitter. The next year he went four innings in relief against the Detroit Tigers but did not figure in the decision.

The big lefty—he's six-five, weighs 210 pounds—began to show his real class in 1969. In September of that year the New York Mets, driving for the National League pennant, faced Carlton at his blinding best. Steve set a major-league record when he fanned nineteen of the New Yorkers, but he lost the game, 4-3, on two home runs by outfielder Ron Swoboda. He won 17 games that year, however, and launched into the first of his salary battles with the Cardinal owner. Carlton eventually signed a contract but then unaccountably had a miserable 1970 season, winning 10 and losing 19.

Steve straightened out in 1971 and had a brilliant 20–7 year, but became deadlocked with Busch over his 1972 contract. The pitcher simply felt he was worth more to the club than Busch did. At the same time the Phillies were having a similar disagreement with their ace, Rick Wise, and the two clubs decided to trade salary problems. Both pitchers got approximately what they were asking for from their new clubs, and the owners presumably saved face. In 1972 Wise, incidentally, won 16 and lost 16 for the Cardinals, a far better team than the Phillies. In that year anyway, the Phils had the better part of the trade.

Carlton got off to a slow start in Philadelphia. By the end of May his record was 5–6. But beginning in the first week in June he was tremendous. His record for the rest of the season was 22–4, with an amazing earned-run average of 1.54. The 15-game winning streak began June 7 with a 3–1 win over Houston and continued until the night of August 21 in Philadelphia.

During that memorable string of victories Steve beat a hard-hitting Pittsburgh club, 2–0, and Pirate slugger Willie Stargell said afterward, "Hitting him tonight was like trying to drink coffee with a fork."

Another Pirate star, the late Roberto Clemente,

was seeking the 3,000th hit of his career when he faced Carlton in a game in Philadelphia. Steve sent him back to Pittsburgh still looking for No. 3,000. A sportswriter asked Carlton if it wouldn't have been an honor to be the pitcher who gave up that hit to Roberto. Steve snapped, "Ask the guy who gives it to him."

On August 17 Carlton went after his fifteenth straight, and No. 20 for the season. It was his wife's birthday and he had promised her a victory. Mrs. Carlton and 53,576 other fans jammed Veterans Stadium to watch Steve work on the powerful Cincinnati Reds, who were coasting to the Western Division championship of the National League. It was not one of Steve's better games, but he won it, 9–4, as his teammates came up with some surprisingly solid hitting. Deron Johnson and Willie Montanez each hit a two-run homer in the Carlton cause.

After the game the fans stayed in their seats and chanted, "We want Steve!" It was an unprecedented display, and the pitcher had to return to the field to acknowledge the thunderous applause.

"It felt great," Steve said later. "Never happened to me before."

In his game story for the Philadelphia *Daily News*, sportswriter Bill Conlin wrote: "He has an intensity and quiet charisma that add fire to his brilliance as a pitcher. The inner strength, which drives him beyond greatness, infects teammates and fans. . . . When he pitches the whole stadium vibrates like a giant cosmic tuning fork."

One reason for Steve's success was his perfect control of three pitches: a blazing fast ball, a big-breaking curve, and a sharp slider. In 1972 he walked only 87 batters in 346⅓ innings.

"Working with Steve is like a day off," said his catcher, John Bateman. "You just get your glove down and he hits it. You know that ball will come in where it's supposed to."

When he lost those 19 games working with St. Louis in 1970, Carlton's critics claimed he had a tendency to lose his concentration in late innings and let ball games slip away that should have been won. With the Phillies, Steve learned to concentrate all the way.

Another reason for his amazing season in the Quaker City is that Steve pitched oftener. When he was with St. Louis, the ace pitcher was Bob Gibson, who worked every five days. The rest of the staff had to conform to Gibson's schedule. Steve has said that at one point with the Cardinals he got only three starts in three weeks; at best he could count on working every fifth or sixth day. At spring training in 1972, Phillies manager Frank Lucchesi talked with Carlton and decided to put him on a four-day rotation. If there was a rainout or an open date with no scheduled game, Steve moved up and pitched ahead of one of the other starters. This kept Carlton busy and happy—and the turnstiles at the ball park from getting rusty.

The regular working schedule also allowed Carlton to build up the right mental attitude for a game. "The day after a start he is perfectly relaxed," general manager Paul Owens told John Flynn. "He's friendly and easygoing. He . . . does his running . . . with the other pitchers. Then he cheerleads for us on the bench.

"The next day he's pretty much the same. But on the third day a change begins to come over him. He begins to withdraw into himself, to concentrate, to get ready. Then on the day that he's scheduled to pitch, he's a different person. He's quiet, intense, and completely within himself. . . . [His] concentration is amazing."

Carlton is generally polite and soft-spoken, but he likes to be left alone. He paid the Phillies for the privilege of rooming alone when the team was on road trips. During the season he lives in Philadelphia with his wife, Beverly, and their two sons, Steve, Jr., and Scott. He also maintains a home in St. Louis.

In the off-season Steve hunts and fishes—sometimes he goes after moose, generally in Canada. Most of his hard-earned money is in real estate; he owns several hundred acres outside St. Louis and other tracts in California and Utah.

Out on the mound Carlton works fast. He doesn't fidget, stare off into space, or scuff up the mound like many other pitchers. He gets the ball, checks the sign from the catcher, and fires to the plate. The whole operation takes about eight seconds.

Steve doesn't know why it should take any longer. "There is nothing to do out there," he says, "except catch the ball and pitch it."

A bronchial disturbance slowed the big southpaw in the spring of 1973 and may have had something to do with his rather disappointing season. He also may have been suffering from the overwork of the 1972 campaign. Although his 1973 won-and-lost record was 13 and 20, he tied Tom Seaver of the Mets for most games completed (18) and Jack Billingham of the Reds for most innings pitched (293), and trailed only Seaver in strike-outs, with 223.

Steve struggled gamely throughout the year and in the last weeks appeared to be regaining his effectiveness. He looked like his old self on September 25 when he held the Pirates, still fighting for a pennant in the last days of the season, to five hits, beating them 2–1 in Pittsburgh.

Baseball people were certain Steve Carlton would be back for more in '74.

Red Powerhouse: Johnny Bench

Baseball's finest catcher since the days of Mickey Cochrane and Bill Dickey may well be the husky young man who guards the plate and pounds the ball out of the park for the Cincinnati Reds. At six-one and 195 pounds, Johnny Bench has the natural ability, speed, power, and desire that can add up to greatness on the diamond.

"He can beat you behind the plate or at the bat," said the manager of the Los Angeles Dodgers, Walter Alston. "In fact, he can ruin you with that bat."

In his first five seasons in the major leagues, Bench

slammed 154 homers while batting in a total of 512 runs. His best year so far was 1970 when he connected for 45 circuit shots. At the start of the 1973 season, Hank Aaron of the Atlanta Braves needed 41 home runs to tie Babe Ruth's career record of 714; some observers were saying that Johnny Bench might beat them both in the years ahead. It's a long shot. Bench, twenty-five years old and a catcher—catchers don't usually play for as many years as outfielders—would have to average $37\frac{1}{3}$ homers for fifteen seasons to tie the Babe. He could possibly do it, though, for Johnny Bench is a mighty ball player.

Besides his potent bat he has a rifle arm that he uses to cut down foolhardy base runners with monotonous regularity. He can snap the ball from beside his right ear, often while still in a crouch. Experts say absolutely nobody can get the ball to second base as quickly and accurately as Johnny. "Johnny Bench takes the running game away from you," one National League coach said. "He sometimes stops runners from running entirely just by his presence behind the plate. The other team has to change basic strategy and it becomes a lot harder to beat his team."

Bench will do things other catchers won't even try. Using a "hinged" glove similar to a first baseman's mitt, he grabs the ball with one hand, keeping his bare hand out of the way (most catchers hold both hands together). On a play at the plate he'll scoop an outfielder's throw out of the dirt like an infielder instead of crouching and using both hands to catch it. This enables him to tag a sliding runner even if the throw to the plate is off target. Then he's in good position to snap the ball to any base.

Bench's fast handling of the ball and his powerful, accurate arm make him the natural key to the Red defense. He has innate speed and catlike reflexes and so can move quickly in his area of operations—jumping out in front of the plate for bunts, controlling errant pitches, backing up first base in case of a wild throw. And Bench is in a class by himself when it comes to blocking the plate against a runner charging in from third. In the ninth inning of the fifth game of the 1972 World Series, John Odom, of the Oakland Athletics, tried to score from third on a short fly. He came down the base line like a runaway express train, crashed into Bench at top speed, was tagged out— and had to be helped to his feet and led off the field. Johnny Bench strolled calmly into the dugout. It was the third out in a 5–4 Cincinnati victory.

His daily heroics for the glory of Cincinnati have won for Johnny Bench the National League's Most Valuable Player award twice in a space of three years. He was the league's starting catcher in the All-Star games of 1969, '70, '71, '72, and '73.

Born on the sixth anniversary of the bombing of Pearl Harbor, December 7, 1947, in Oklahoma City, John Lee Bench was the third of four children of Ted Bench, owner of a small trucking business, and his wife, Katie. One of his father's grandparents was a member of the Choctaw tribe, making Johnny one-eighth Indian. When he was four years old the family moved to the rural community of Binger, Oklahoma, where Johnny was soon supplementing the meager family income by picking cotton and peanuts in the fields, mowing lawns, and delivering newspapers.

His father had been a semi-pro catcher, and so it's not surprising that the Benches found time to play baseball. Ted Bench taught the boy everything he knew and was instrumental in developing the powerful throwing arm that helped make Johnny a great catcher in the years to come.

He was good at all sports, starring on the school's basketball team and later becoming a fine golfer and bowler. But life wasn't all fun and games. Johnny was a thoughtful youngster and a good student. He graduated first in his high-school class.

Baseball scouts became interested in Johnny because of his strong arm and robust hitting. He was selected by Cincinnati in the June, 1965, draft and told to concentrate on catching.

The Reds sent the boy to Tampa, of the Florida State League, and he moved right up the ladder. In 1966 he was with Peninsula, of the Carolina League, and halfway through the season he made the big jump to Buffalo, of the International League. Toward the close of the 1967 season he was brought up to the parent club and installed as the Reds' No. 1 catcher.

He was nineteen years old when he turned up in a Cincinnati uniform, and he was an instant hit with the Red fans. In 1968 he hit a solid .275 and was named National League Rookie of the Year. The next year Johnny upped his average to .293, with 26 homers and 90 runs batted in.

In 1970 the Big Red Machine, hitting on all cylinders, crushed the Western Division, ran over the Pirates in three straight in the National League pennant play-offs, and rumbled into the World Series with the Baltimore Orioles. The young catcher had a sensational year, again batting .293, with 45 homers and 148 RBI's. In one four-game series with the St. Louis Cardinals, Bench had ten hits, six of them homers, and knocked in fourteen runs. The Cardinals were happy to leave Cincinnati. "He shocks you," said Red Schoendienst, Cardinal manager. Bench, of course, received the National League's Most Valuable Player award.

The Machine had engine trouble in the World Series, however, and ground to a halt as the Orioles won in five games. Cincinnati's power was effectively checked by high-grade Oriole pitching, while Baltimore batters hit Red pitching with considerable abandon. The star of the Series was the Orioles' Brooks Robinson, who batted .450 and repeatedly robbed the Reds of base hits with his brilliant play at third base.

Although the World Series was a big disappointment, Johnny Bench, on the strength of his fine season, took off on a series of speaking engagements at banquets throughout the country. He also toured a war zone with comedian Bob Hope and conducted his own television show. It was all very exciting for the youngster from Binger, Oklahoma, but it left him physically and emotionally drained and led to a dismal 1971 season. His batting average skidded to .238, a career low, and he hit only 27 homers and knocked in but 61 runs. Worse, the Red team stumbled all the way to a fourth-place tie with Houston.

The Reds were sluggish through most of the season, but they managed to put on a drive right at the end that almost scrambled the league. Cincinnati won 16 of its last 20 games against the top teams— Pittsburgh, St. Louis, Chicago, San Francisco, and Los Angeles. But the charge came much too late, and the Reds finished 11 games behind the winning San Francisco Giants.

Cincinnati manager Sparky Anderson put his deflated heroes through a rough spring training session in 1972, but even so Johnny Bench and his mates got off to a slow start. The big catcher was hitting around .200 when the club pulled into the Houston Astrodome for a four-game series. It was a turning point. Bench banged four homers and the Reds swept the set.

Johnny Bench continued to make the ball bleed. Early in June he slammed seven homers in five games to tie a National League record set some forty years before by "Sunny Jim" Bottomley, a St. Louis Cardinal first baseman. The Big Red Machine moved into first place June 25 and stayed there. The Western Division title was officially clinched September 22 with a 4–3 victory in Houston. The winning run was Johnny Bench's thirty-seventh homer of the season. Five days later he hit No. 40 for the benefit of the Cincinnati fans.

The World Champions of 1971, the Pittsburgh Pirates, easily conquered the National League's Eastern Division and engaged the Reds in a thrill-packed pennant play-off struggle that went the five-game limit. With the teams tied at two games apiece, the Pirates held a 3–2 lead going into the last half of the ninth inning at Cincinnati. Johnny Bench was the first man up, and Pirate pitcher Dave Giusti had orders to keep the ball on the outside of the plate so the powerful right-handed hitter couldn't pull anything to deep left field. What happened was that the pitch came over the outside all right, but Johnny Bench, with power to burn in any direction, hit over the right-field wall, tying the score at 3–3. Then the Reds took the ball game, and the pennant, on two singles and a wild pitch by another Pirate pitcher, Bob Moose.

The Oakland A's, victors over Detroit in the American League play-offs, took their mustached heroes into Cincinnati's Riverfront Stadium to start the World Series. Ace Oakland hurlers Ken Holtzman and Catfish Hunter choked off the Red hitters to win the first two games, 3–2 and 2–1. They were so effective that they were able to keep the first three

Red batters hitless; hence the clean-up hitter, Johnny Bench, was always coming up with the bases bare. The thinking behind this, of course, was that even if Bench did hit one into the seats, it couldn't hurt too much with nobody on base ahead of him.

A fine clutch effort by the right-handed pitcher Jack Billingham, who posted a 1–0 victory in the third game, put the Reds back in contention. But Johnny Bench's face still turns crimson when he thinks about one incident in this game. In the eighth inning Cincinnati had men on second and third with one out. Bench was the batter, and Oakland pitcher Rollie Fingers ran the count to three and two.

That's when Oakland got a little sneaky. Manager Dick Williams trotted out to talk to Fingers, and on his way back to the dugout he nodded. Oakland catcher Gene Tenace pointed toward first, the usual sign for an intentional walk; he also took a half step toward the outside of the plate. Joe Morgan, the Red runner on third, sensed something was going on and yelled to Bench to watch out.

Johnny, relaxed and ready to drop his bat and trot to first base, heard Morgan—but not in time. Fingers fired a slider over the outside corner of the plate for strike three.

"I heard Morgan yell at me," a shamefaced Bench said later. "But Fingers made a very good pitch. He caught me looking."

Oakland bounced back to take the fourth game and a commanding two-game lead in the Series, but then the Reds rallied to take two in a row, 5–4 and 8–1, to tie everything up. Bench's lone homer of the Series came in the sixth game and broke a scoreless tie. Then the Reds went on to win the game easily.

The Series finale was another heart-stopping squeaker. In the eighth inning the Reds, trailing 3–1, put runners on second and third. Johnny Bench was up. Now, it's axiomatic in baseball that you don't put the potential winning run on base purposely. But the A's did just that, walking Bench and skirting the extra-base danger in his power-laden bat.

Actually Cincinnati did get one run in the inning on a sacrifice fly—but lost the game, 3–2, and the championship, four games to three. Throughout the Series, Dick Williams had managed the Oakland club astutely. Of course, he had some unexpected help. Joe Rudi's unbelievable catch that saved the second game, and the unlooked-for slugging of catcher Gene Tenace, contributed heavily to the Oakland victory. Tenace banged out four homers and knocked in nine runs while compiling a .348 batting average.

Johnny Bench and his teammates had something to think about. Twice in three years they had been beaten in the fall classic. Oakland pitchers had held Bench to six hits in 23 times at bat. He scored four runs and had only one run batted in. Behind the plate, however, he functioned normally, cutting down four Oakland runners trying to steal second. The A's, a running team during the season, didn't take many chances on Bench's arm.

Johnny Bench won the 1972 Most Valuable Player award, but it turned out that he had been playing all season with a tumor on one lung. He underwent surgery in Cincinnati and subsequent tests proved the tumor benign. In fact he was discharged from the hospital four days after the operation. But while he was there, the handsome, personable young star broke a hospital record when he averaged more than 2,000 get-well letters a day. Fans throughout the nation were concerned.

Although he lives in a deluxe bachelor apartment, drives big cars, and likes music and pretty girls, John somehow manages to remain a loner.

"It makes me nervous having a lot of people around all the time," he told Bill Libby, author of a biography of Bench. "But I like to be around the family," he added. "Maybe it's because they take me as I am. I don't have to prove anything to them." In 1969 Johnny was engaged to an airline stewardess, but the two drifted apart. He dates a lot, and friends say he would like to be married and have a family. For the time being, however, he'll settle for being the best catcher in baseball.

The 1973 Reds won more games in the regular season (99) than any team in either league and coasted to victory in the Western Division of the National League. Johnny Bench, hitting .253, slugged out 25 home runs and sent 104 runs across the plate.

Bench's ninth-inning home run won the first game of the play-off series with the Mets, winners in the

Eastern Division, but excellent New York pitching pretty much throttled the Red attack after that. The Mets won three of the next four games and went into the World Series against the Athletics. In addition to his home run, Bench had two singles and two doubles in the play-off series.

What's ahead for the Reds' great young star? Well, Ted Williams, famed slugger of another era, wrote on a baseball: "To Johnny Bench, a Hall of Famer for sure." Most baseball people agree—Johnny Bench can't miss.

Index

Aaron, Hank (Henry Louis), 163, 219–229
  on All-Star team, 220
  batting championship won by, 226
  boyhood of, 221–222
  with Braves, 222, 223–229
  minor-league career of, 222–223
  Most Valuable Player award won by, 220, 224
  and home-run record, lifetime, 219–220, 227, 228–229, 253
  records of, 220, 222, 223, 224, 225–226, 227–228, 229
  in World Series, 220, 224–226
Abrams, Cal, 180
Adcock, Joe, 163, 224, 225, 227
Alexander, Grover Cleveland, 40 41, 181, 243
Allen, Mel, 127
All-Star games, 62, 63, 85–86, 113, 129, 140, 141–142, 196, 209, 220, 236, 254
American League, 1, 3, 7, 8, 22, 25, 46, 49, 61, 85, 113, 117, 118, 128, 140, 145–146,

American League (*cont.*)
149, 154, 165, 186, 193, 194, 215
Antonelli, Johnny, 175, 214, 215
Ashburn, Richie, 140, 180, 185, 187, 188
Athletics, *see* Oakland Athletics; Philadelphia Athletics
Atlanta Braves, 219, 220, 227, 228, 229
Averill, Earl, 113, 130

Baker Bowl (Philadelphia), 39
Baltimore Orioles, 21, 47, 238–239, 256
Baseball Hall of Fame, *see* Hall of Fame
batting championship, *see* Aaron; Clemente; Cobb; DiMaggio, Joe; Gehrig; Heilmann; Hornsby; Mantle; Mays; Musial; Robinson, Jackie; Ruth; Simmons; Sisler, George; Speaker; Walker; Williams, Ted
"Battle of St. Louis," 96, 111
Bench, Johnny (John Lee), 240, 252–262
  in All-Star games, 254
  fielding ability of, 253–254
  life style of, 261
  minor-league career of, 255
  Most Valuable Player award won by, 254, 256, 261
  records of, 252–253, 254, 256, 257, 261, 262
  with Reds, 255–262
  surgery on, 261

Bench, Johnny (*cont.*)
  in World Series, 254, 256, 259, 260
  youth of, 254–255
Bench, Ted, 254, 255
Berra, Yogi, 204, 213
Billingham, Jack, 251, 259
Bishop, Max, 58, 59, 67
Black Sox Scandal (1919), 18
Blass, Steve, 231–232, 239
"blooper" ball, 142
Boston Braves, 30, 45, 118–120, 158, 159, 160, 161, 162, 163, 189–190
Boston Red Sox, 21, 22, 117, 118, 125–126, 152
Bottomley, "Sunny Jim," 257
Boudreau, Lou, 119, 159
"Boudreau shift," 143, 147
Braves, *see* Atlanta Braves; Boston Braves; Milwaukee Braves
Breadon, Sam, 36, 38, 43
Brecheen, Harry, 152
Bridges, Tommy, 64, 109
Briggs, Walter O., 70–71
Brooklyn Dodgers, 22, 30, 33, 93–94, 106, 133, 135, 150, 151–152, 167, 168, 171, 172–175, 176, 179–181, 185–186, 191–192, 202, 203, 208, 211, 212–213, 233
Brown, Mordecai, 8
Browns, *see* St. Louis Browns
Burdette, Lew, 157, 163, 164, 224, 225, 226
Busch, Gussie, 242, 247

INDEX

Campanella, Roy, 155, 172, 192
Cardinals, *see* St. Louis Cardinals
Carlton, Steve (Steven Norman), 242–251
   boyhood of, 244–245
   with Cardinals, 245, 246–247, 249
   character of, 244, 248–249, 250
   minor-league career of, 245–246
   with Phillies, 242–244, 247–251
   pitching style of, 250–251
   records of, 243, 246–247, 248, 249, 251
   in World Series, 246
Chesbro, Jack, 6
Chicago Cubs, 8, 18, 22, 45–46, 56–58, 70, 81, 91, 110, 111, 114–116
Chicago White Sox, 18, 62
Cincinnati Reds, 18, 47, 218, 238, 240, 252, 254, 255, 256, 257, 260, 261–262
Clemente, Roberto, 230–241, 247–248
   in All-Star game, 236
   base running of, 234–235
   batting championship won by, 236, 237
   death of, 230–231, 240
   early life of, 232–233
   fielding ability of, 231–232
   to Hall of Fame, election of, 240–241
   marriage of, 237
Clemente, Roberto (*cont.*)
   Most Valuable Player award won by, 238
   with Pirates, 233–240
   records of, 231, 236, 237, 238, 239
   in World Series, 231, 236, 238, 239
Cleveland Indians, 27, 52–53, 117–118, 120, 123–124, 125–126, 129–131, 132, 135, 136, 158–159, 162, 208, 215
Cobb, Ty (Tyrus Raymond), 1–4, 15, 21, 54, 66, 228
   with Athletics, 14
   batting championship won by, 6–7, 9, 10, 11, 12
   boyhood of, 5
   character of, 2–3, 10–11
   early baseball career of, 5–6
   to Hall of Fame, election of, 14
   records of, 2, 5, 6–7, 8, 9, 10, 11, 12, 13, 14
   in retirement, 15–16
   strike of players caused by, 11–12
   with Tigers, 6–14
   in World Series, 8–10
Cochrane, Mickey (Gordon Stanley), 49, 50, 52, 53, 55, 56, 57, 58, 62–71, 252
   in All-Star game, 63
   with Athletics, 62–64, 65–69
   at Boston University, 64–65
   injury to, 70
   minor-league career of, 65

Cochrane, Mickey (*cont.*)
  Most Valuable Player award won by, 63
  records of, 63, 68
  in retirement, 70–71
  with Tigers, 69–71
  in World Series, 64, 68–69, 70
Conlin, Bill, 248–249
Crawford, Sam, 7, 21
Cronin, Joe, 86, 145
Crosetti, Frank, 115–116, 132–133
Cubs, *see* Chicago Cubs

Dark, Alvin, 211, 213
Dean, Dizzy (Jerome Herman), 92, 94, 96, 99–116, 123, 182
  in All-Star games, 113
  boyhood of, 101–102
  with Cardinals, 102–114
  with Cubs, 114–116
  injury to, 100, 113–114
  marriage of, 104
  minor-league career of, 102, 103–104, 116
  Most Valuable Player award won by, 110
  as radio sportscaster, 100–101, 116
  records of, 100, 104, 111, 123
  suspension of, 111–112
  in World Series, 108, 109–110, 115–116
Dean, Paul, 94, 105–106, 108, 109, 111
  no-hitter by, 107
Detroit Tigers, 6, 7–9, 62, 69–70, 108–110

Dickey, Bill, 78, 82, 86, 132, 252
DiMaggio, Joe, 74, 78, 82, 122, 127–137, 142, 195
  in All-Star game, 129
  in Army Air Forces, 134
  batting championship won by, 128, 131
  character of, 128
  early baseball career of, 128
  to Hall of Fame, election of, 137
  injuries to, 137
  marriage of, 131
  Most Valuable Player award won by, 128, 135
  records of, 128, 129, 131–132, 134, 135
  retirement of, 137
  salary of, 131
  in World Series, 116, 187, 201
  with Yankees, 129–137
DiMaggio, Vince, 113
Dodgers, *see* Brooklyn Dodgers; Los Angeles Dodgers
"dropkick" play, 213–214
Dunn, Jack, 21

Earnshaw, George, 60, 61, 67, 81
Ebbets Field (Brooklyn), 33, 167, 171, 175, 178, 179, 186, 202, 212
Ehmke, Howard, 68
Ennis, Del, 165, 188, 190
"ephus" ball, 142

fadeaway pitch, 88
Feller, Bob (Robert), 117–126, 136, 148

INDEX

Feller, Bob (*cont.*)
  boyhood of, 122-123
  financial acumen of, 120-121, 126
  with Indians, 123-126
  in Navy, 124
  no-hitters by, 118, 121-122, 124, 126
  one-hitters by, 124, 125, 126
  records of, 118, 123, 124, 125
  retirement of, 126
  strike-out ability of, 123, 124
  in World Series, 118-120
Fenway Park (Boston), 142
Fingers, Rollie, 259
Forbes Field (Pittsburgh), 37, 220, 232
Ford, Whitey, 22, 164, 225
Fournier, Jake, 33-34
Foxx, Jimmy, 55, 57, 58, 60, 61, 86, 103, 203, 228
Frazee, Harry, 22-23
Frick, Ford, 111, 112
Frisch, Frankie, 43, 105, 106, 108, 109, 110

"Gashouse Gang," 69, 105, 106, 109, 110, 114
Gehrig, Lou (Louis), 23, 40, 41, 72-84, 86, 128, 228
  and Babe Ruth, 72-73, 77, 79-80
  boyhood of, 74-75
  character of, 74, 79, 84
  at Columbia University, 76
  death of, 84
  home-run hitting of, 73, 75, 76, 78, 79, 80-81, 83
  marriage of, 79

Gehrig, Lou (*cont.*)
  minor-league career of, 77-78
  and multiple sclerosis, 74, 83
  records of, 73-74, 78, 80, 81-83
  in World Series, 73-74, 78, 80, 81
  with Yankees, 76, 78-84
Giants, *see* New York Giants; San Francisco Giants
Gordon, Joe, 132, 133, 141
Greenberg, Hank, 110, 203
Greenwade, Tom, 199
Griffith Stadium (Washington), 195
Grove, Lefty, 20, 52, 55, 57, 67, 165, 243

Haas, Mule, 55, 57, 58, 59, 62, 67
Haines, Jesse, 39, 40, 41, 42, 93
Hall of Fame (Cooperstown), 14, 33, 47, 62, 137, 166, 177, 241
Hartnett, Gabby, 91, 115
Hearn, Jim, 185, 211, 212
Heilmann, Harry, 13, 54, 55, 67, 145
Henrich, Tommy, 122, 130, 132, 133
Hodges, Gil, 155, 172, 181, 191
Hornsby, Rogers, 32-48
  and baseball school for boys, 47
  batting championship won by, 36, 45
  batting style of, 34, 35-36
  boyhood of, 34-35
  with Braves, 45

Hornsby, Rogers (*cont.*)
  with Browns, 46–47
  with Cardinals, 35–43, 46
  character of, 32–33, 44
  with Cubs, 45–46
  death of, 48
  with Giants, 43–44
  to Hall of Fame, election of, 33, 47
  as manager, 38–43, 45–47
  minor-league career of, 35, 47
  as newspaperman and sportscaster, 47
  with Orioles, 47
  records of, 33, 35, 37, 38, 44, 45, 46
  with Reds, 47
  in World Series, 39, 40, 41, 42, 45
Hubbell, Carl, 85–98, 111, 112, 243
  in All-Star game, 85–86
  boyhood of, 87–88
  character of, 96–97
  with Giants, 86–87, 90–98
  minor-league career of, 88, 89
  no-hitter by, 87, 91
  records of, 86–87, 91–92, 93, 97
  retirement of, 98
  and screwball, 88
  with Tigers, 88–89
  in World Series, 93, 95, 96
Huggins, Miller, 24, 26, 77

Indians, *see* Cleveland Indians
Irvin, Monte, 211, 212, 213

Jackson, "Shoeless Joe," 10–11
Jennings, Hughie, 12, 13
Johnson, Ban, 12
Johnson, Walter, 118

Keeler, Willie, 131–132
Keller, Charley, 122
Keltner, Ken, 126, 132, 141, 142
Kiner, Ralph, 153
Kinsella, Dick, 89
Konstanty, Dick, 185, 186, 188, 192
Krichell, Paul, 76

Lajoie, Larry, 10
Larsen, Don, 176–177, 203
Lockman, Whitey, 211, 213
Logan, Johnny, 163, 165, 189, 190, 224
Los Angeles Dodgers, 175, 216

Mack, Connie, 14, 49, 51, 52, 54, 57, 60, 62, 63–64, 65, 66, 68, 69
Mantle, Mickey, 194–206
  in All-Star games, 196
  batting championship won by, 203
  boyhood of, 196–199
  home-run hitting of, 195, 196, 200, 201, 202, 203, 204, 205
  injuries to, 198, 201, 205
  marriage of, 204
  Most Valuable Player award won by, 195
  records of, 195–196, 202, 203, 204, 205
  retirement of, 205–206
  strike-out problem of, 196, 200, 201–202

INDEX

Mantle, Mickey (*cont.*)
   as switch hitter, 197
   Triple Crown won by, 196, 203
   in World Series, 195–196, 201, 202–203, 205
   with Yankees, 199–206
Maris, Roger, 27, 196, 220
Marquard, Rube, 243
Martin, Billy, 174, 204
Martin, Pepper, 69, 105–106
Masi, Phil, 119
Mathews, Eddie, 163, 165, 190, 224, 225, 227
Mathewson, Christy, 88
Mays, Willie, 175, 207–218
   in All-Star game, 209
   in Army, 214
   batting championship won by, 214
   boyhood of, 209
   with Giants, 207–209, 211–217
   with Mets, 217–218
   minor-league career of, 209–210
   Most Valuable Player award won by, 208, 217
   records of, 214, 215, 216, 217
   retirement of, 217–218
   skills of, 207–208
   in World Series, 201, 208, 213, 215, 216, 218
Mazeroski, Bill, 235, 236
McCarthy, Joe, 46, 82, 83, 94–95
McGraw, John, 26, 43, 44, 89–91
Mets, *see* New York Mets

Meusel, Bob, 41, 42, 78
Miller, Bing, 52, 53, 55, 57, 58
Milwaukee Braves, 156, 157, 163–164, 204, 220, 222, 223, 226
Mize, Johnny, 153
Moon, Wally, 223
Morgan, Joe, 259
Most Valuable Player award, *see* Aaron; Bench; Clemente; Cochrane; Dean, Dizzy; DiMaggio, Joe; Mantle; Mays; Musial; Robinson, Jackie; Williams, Ted
Municipal Stadium (Cleveland), 136
"Murderers' Row," 78
Musial, Stan (Stanley), 138, 139, 149–154, 155, 188, 216, 228
   in All-Star games, 140
   batting championship won by, 140, 150–151, 153
   batting style of, 140
   with Cardinals, 150–154
   fielding ability of, 141
   marriage of, 153
   minor-league career of, 149–150
   Most Valuable Player award won by, 140–141, 151, 153
   in Navy, 151
   records of, 150–151, 152, 153, 154
   in World Series, 146, 150, 151

National League, 9, 33, 36, 37, 56, 73, 85, 111, 113, 129, 140, 141, 153, 159, 163,

National League (*cont.*) 172, 173, 207, 209, 218, 220, 236, 237, 246, 254, 256, 258
Negro American League, 222
Newcombe, Don, 179, 185
New York Giants, 25, 26, 83, 86–87, 89–90, 91–95, 96, 97, 98, 111, 172, 173, 174–175, 201, 207, 208, 209, 210, 211–212, 213, 214–215, 216–217
New York Mets, 217–218, 246
New York Yankees, 19, 25, 40–43, 54, 55–56, 67, 70, 73–74, 94–95, 96, 115–116, 117, 121–122, 129–131, 132, 133–134, 135–136, 150, 157, 164–166, 171–172, 173–174, 175, 176, 186–188, 194, 196, 199, 201, 202, 203, 204, 205, 213–214, 216–217, 224–225, 235–236
no-hitters, *see* Dean, Paul; Feller; Hubbell; Larsen; Pearson

Oakland Athletics, 218, 258–259
Orioles, *see* Baltimore Orioles
Ott, Mel, 93
Owen, Mickey, 133

Parmalee, Roy, 93, 94
Pearson, Monte, 131
Pennock, Herb, 40
Philadelphia Athletics, 5, 7–8, 9, 20, 45–46, 49, 65, 67, 81, 103, 117

Philadelphia Phillies, 39, 179–181, 184–192, 211, 242, 243, 244, 246, 247, 248, 249–250
Pipp, Wallie, 24, 77, 78
Pittsburgh Pirates, 9, 39, 90, 91, 103, 114–115, 226, 230, 231, 233–236, 238–240, 258
Plank, Eddie, 165
Podres, Johnny, 175, 234
Polo Grounds (New York), 24, 39, 85, 92, 95, 208, 211
Pride of the Yankees, 84
Pruett, Hub, 25
Puerto Rico, 230

Raschi, Vic, 186–187
Reach Baseball Guide, 25, 38–39
Reds, *see* Cincinnati Reds
Red Sox, *see* Boston Red Sox
Reese, Peewee, 173, 174, 180
Rhodes, Dusty, 215
Rickey, Branch, 37, 38, 169, 170–171, 172
Riddle, Chase, 245
Riverfront Stadium (Cincinnati), 177, 258
Rizzuto, Phil, 213–214
Roberts, Robin, 173, 179–193
  with Astros, 193
  at Michigan State, 183–184
  with Orioles, 193
  with Phillies, 184–193
  pitching abilities of, 181–183
  records of, 181, 182, 183, 188–189, 191, 192
  in World Series, 187, 188

INDEX

Robertson, Bob, 238, 239
Robinson, Brooks, 256
Robinson, Jackie (Jack Roosevelt), 167–178, 181, 223–224
  in Army, 170
  boyhood of, 169–170
  character of, 168–169, 171, 172, 173
  death of, 178
  with Dodgers, 171–177
  as first black major-league player, 167–168
  to Hall of Fame, election of, 177
  marriage and family of, 176, 177
  military career of, 170
  minor-league career of, 170–171
  Most Valuable Player award won by, 168, 172
  records of, 168, 172, 175
  in retirement, 177–178
  at UCLA, 170
  in World Series, 174, 175, 176
Root, Charlie, 18, 45, 57
Ruffing, Red (Charlie), 54, 82, 95
Ruppert, Jake, 27, 29
Ruth, Babe (George Herman), 16–31, 72, 74, 77, 78, 82, 86, 139
  batting championship won by, 26
  boyhood of, 21
  with Braves, 30
  death of, 30–31
  with Dodgers, 30

Ruth, Babe (*cont.*)
  home-run hitting by, 17, 18, 20–21, 22, 23, 24, 25, 26, 27, 28, 30, 40, 41, 55, 61, 79, 203, 219, 220, 228, 229, 253
  life style of, 16–17, 23–25, 26, 28
  marriage of, 19
  with Orioles, 21
  as pitcher, 21–22
  records of, 17, 22, 23, 25, 26, 27, 28, 61, 79, 196, 203, 219, 220, 228, 229, 253
  with Red Sox, 21–23
  retirement of, 30
  salary of, 19, 28, 121
  suspension of, 26–27
  in World Series, 18, 22, 27, 28, 40, 41, 42
  with Yankees, 23–30

Sain, Johnny, 118–119, 161–162
St. Louis Browns, 10, 32, 46–47, 125, 151
St. Louis Cardinals, 27, 32, 33, 36, 37, 38, 39, 40–43, 61, 69–70, 78, 80, 92, 146, 151–152, 171, 224
San Francisco Giants, 216, 238
screwball pitch, 88, 89, 96
Seaver, Tom, 251
Senators, *see* Washington Senators
Sewell, Rip, 142
Shea Stadium (Queens), 217
Shibe Park (Philadelphia), 3, 14, 20, 52, 53, 62, 67, 181, 185, 189

Simmons, Al (Aloysius Harry Szymanski), 49, 50–62, 81, 86, 103
  on All-Star teams, 62
  with Athletics, 51–62
  batting championship won by, 61
  batting stance of, 51
  boyhood of, 50
  to Hall of Fame, election of, 62
  with Indians, 62
  injury to, 60
  minor-league career of, 50–51
  records of, 52, 54, 55, 56, 61, 62
  with Reds, 62
  with Red Sox, 62
  retirement of, 62
  with Tigers, 62
  with White Sox, 62
  in World Series, 56, 61
Sisler, Dick, 181, 188
Sisler, George, 13
Slaughter, Enos, 150, 152
Smith, Red, 173
Snider, Duke, 172, 173, 174, 175, 180
Southworth, Billy, 161
Spahn, Warren Edward, 156–166, 224
  in Army, 160
  boyhood of, 159–160
  with Braves, 161–166
  character of, 156–157, 158
  to Hall of Fame, election of, 166
  marriage of, 160–161
  minor-league career of, 160

Spahn, Warren Edward (*cont.*)
  pitching style of, 162–163
  records of, 157–158, 161, 162, 165, 166
  in World Series, 158–159, 164–165, 165–166, 225, 226
Speaker, Tris, 12, 54
Sporting News, The, 154, 203
Sportsman's Park (St. Louis), 100
Stanky, Eddie, 119, 211, 213–214
Stargell, Willie, 228, 231, 238, 239, 247
Stengel, Casey, 174, 196, 199, 200
Street, Gabby, 103
Sukeforth, Clyde, 170
Swoboda, Ron, 246

Tenace, Gene, 259, 260
Terry, Bill, 93, 113
Thomas, Frank, 227, 234
Thomson, Bobby, 211, 212, 223
  historic home run by, 173, 201, 213, 221
Three Rivers Stadium (Pittsburgh), 231, 238
Tigers, *see* Detroit Tigers

Vance, Dazzy, 38
Veach, Bobby, 13, 21
Veeck, Bill, 47
Veterans Stadium (Philadelphia), 244, 248

Walker, Dixie, 151

INDEX

Ward, Chuck, 184
Warlick, H. L., 34
Washington Senators, 53, 58–60, 93, 194–195
White Sox, *see* Chicago White Sox
"Whiz Kids," 185, 186
Williams, Dick, 259, 260
Williams, Ted, 138, 141–149, 204, 262
  in All-Star games, 141–142
  batting championship won by, 145, 147, 154
  batting style of, 139–140
  minor-league career of, 143–144
  Most Valuable Player award won by, 148
  in Navy Air Corps, 145–146, 149
  records of, 144–145, 146, 147–148, 154
  with Red Sox, 144–149, 154–155
  retirement of, 154
  unpopularity of, 146–147
  in World Series, 146
Wise, Rick, 247
World Series:
  1907, 1908 (Cubs–Tigers), 8
  1909 (Pirates–Tigers), 9
  1916 (Red Sox–Dodgers), 22
  1918 (Red Sox–Cubs), 22
  1919 (Reds–White Sox), 18
  1922 (Giants–Yankees), 25
  1923 (Yankees–Giants), 26
  1926 (Cardinals–Yankees), 27, 40–43, 78
  1928 (Yankees–Cardinals),

World Series (*cont.*)
  28, 73–74, 80
  1929 (Athletics–Cubs), 45–46, 56–58, 68
  1930 (Athletics–Cardinals), 61, 68
  1931 (Cardinals–Athletics), 61, 68–69
  1932 (Yankees–Cubs), 18, 81
  1933 (Giants–Senators), 93
  1934 (Cardinals–Tigers), 69, 108–109
  1935 (Tigers–Cubs), 64, 70
  1936 (Yankees–Giants), 94–95
  1937 (Yankees–Giants), 83, 96
  1938 (Yankees–Cubs), 115–116
  1941 (Yankees–Dodgers), 133
  1942 (Cardinals–Yankees), 150
  1944 (Cardinals–Browns), 151
  1946 (Cardinals–Red Sox), 146, 152
  1947 (Yankees–Dodgers), 135
  1948 (Indians–Braves), 118–120, 158–159, 162
  1950 (Yankees–Phillies), 186–188
  1951 (Yankees–Giants), 201, 213–214
  1952 (Yankees–Dodgers), 174, 202
  1953 (Yankees–Dodgers), 174, 202–203

World Series (*cont.*)
  1954 (Giants–Indians), 215
  1955 (Dodgers–Yankees), 175
  1956 (Yankees–Dodgers), 176, 203
  1957 (Braves–Yankees), 164–165, 204, 224–226
  1958 (Yankees–Braves), 165–166, 205, 226
  1960 (Pirates–Yankees), 235–236
  1961 (Yankees–Reds), 22
  1962 (Yankees–Giants), 216–217
  1970 (Orioles–Reds), 256

World Series (*cont.*)
  1971 (Pirates–Orioles), 238–239
  1972 (Athletics–Reds), 258–259
  1973 (Athletics–Mets), 218
Wrigley, Phil, 38, 114
Wrigley Field (Chicago), 75–76
Wyatt, Whit, 133

Yankees, *see* New York Yankees
Yankee Stadium (Bronx), 15, 25, 55, 73, 127, 132, 146, 164, 175, 225

About the Author

Robert Shoemaker, now a free-lance writer, was associated with *This Week* magazine in New York for almost twenty-five years. Later he joined the staff of the Philadelphia *Daily News.* He obtained his early newspaper experience with the Pottstown (Pennsylvania) *Mercury*, where he covered "everything from sports, fires, and fights to meetings of the Ladies Aid Society."

A native of Pottstown, Mr. Shoemaker was graduated from the Hill School and Pennsylvania State University. He now lives in Tyrone, Pennsylvania.